Shoebox Funeral

Stories from Wolf Creek

Elisabeth Voltz

SHOEBOX FUNERAL

STORIES FROM WOLF CREEK

✳✳✳ BY ✳✳✳

ELISABETH VOLTZ

ILLUSTRATIONS BY IDIL GÖZDE

SHOEBOX FUNERAL
STORIES FROM WOLF CREEK

Edited by Christina M. Frey

Illustrated & Designed by Idil Gözde

Copyright © 2017 by Elisabeth Voltz

Animal Media Group books may be ordered through Consortium Book Sales & Distribution Company or contacting:

ANIMAL MEDIA GROUP
100 First Avenue, Suite 1100, Pittsburgh, PA 15222

animalmediagroup.com
412-566-5656

The views expressed in this work are solely those of the author and do not necessarily reflect the view of the publisher, and the publisher here disclaims any responsibility for them.

FIRST EDITION APRIL 2017

ISBN: 978-0-9861489-5-8
e-book: 978-0-9861489-6-5

IN LOVING MEMORY OF PETER, WITHOUT WHOM WE

WOULD NEVER HAVE COME TO THE FARM.

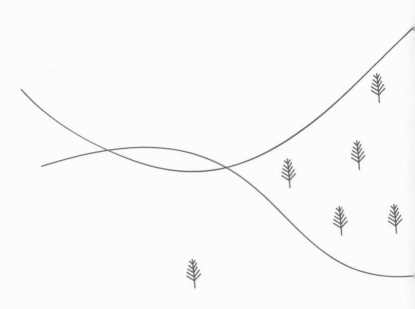

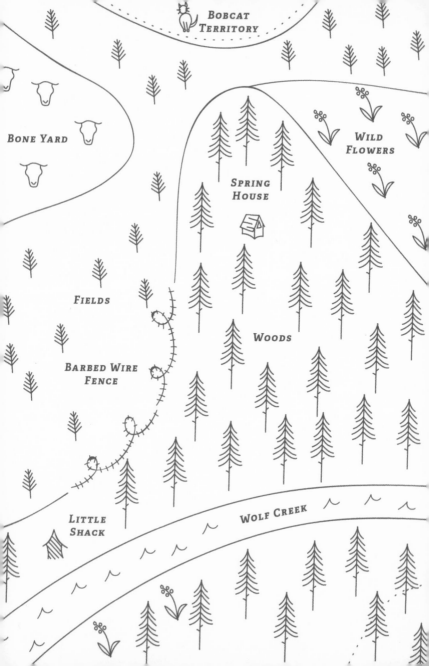

FOREWORD

*T*hese memories are based on a small transitioning farm in the 1980s and 1990s in rural Pennsylvania. Animals still existed not for enjoyment but for purpose—and if an animal didn't serve their purpose, they did not survive the people or the environment, much less the winters. I remember neighboring farmers talking about drowning a bag of cats in the creek or shooting an old horse, which gave me nightmares at a young age. But that was simply the harsh reality of farm life. There was not enough money to cover extra animals, and there was no access to spaying and neutering.

Veterinarian care was a luxury reserved for the milk cows, the "cash cows."

It is easy to look down on this today, to consider it uneducated or evil, but the world we live in now did not exist until recently. This was the nature of the struggle for survival on a poor farm—and a lingering echo of early America and the Depression, something that still lived on in small pockets of Appalachia.

And that made petlike animals like dogs and cats extremely precious to us young kids. Because these "useless" creatures were barely tolerated by the more pragmatic adults, most of our animal friendships were secret—an escape world where we could protect and maintain our furry friends. We would sneak extra food to them, build them makeshift houses and tunnels from hay bales, and hide them from getting dropped off in the woods. At times we felt like the French resistance of World War II, a secret society bound to protect our beloved dogs and cats.

I suppose it's a testament to Mom's love of nature that's embedded in all of us, but as we grew older, the farm slowly became kinder, shifting from a harsh survival workplace to more of a hospice for needy animals looking for a safe place to spend their last years. I'd like to think it was the quiet, secret influence of us kids over time. No matter how much we tried to hide it, Mom and Dad saw us protect and care for our many pets—and as the years passed, they quietly rewarded us when the opportunity presented itself in the form of another hard-luck case in need of saving.

— *Ray Voltz Jr., March 2017*

SHOEBOX FUNERAL

STORIES FROM WOLF CREEK

ELISABETH VOLTZ

SMALL BOXES

Wolf Creek winds like a snake through the woods and under the rusty iron bridge marking the entrance to our farm. Fallen trees crisscross the shallow creek, and the smell of the muddy bank still fills the air. To us as children, this spot was the end of civilization, the land transitioning from cultivated space to the untamed wilds of the swamp—a place of beauty but romanticized danger as well. And here, on the wooded hillside facing this world of in between, not quite real and not quite fantasy, we buried favorite animals and marked their graves with handmade wooden crosses bearing their names.

The hillside faced east toward the rising sun, as is traditional for cemeteries, and it was surrounded by an aura of peace. The land was covered in a wild orchard grass that grew twelve inches high each spring yet remained delicate and wispy—soft to walk through. We planted *Lamiastrum*, or archangel, which eventually intermixed with the witch hazel thickets planted by the frontiersmen before us. Down closer to the marsh were buttercups, marsh marigold, and skunkweed, and though the soil where we dug graves was sandy, it was littered with small, rounded stones, the product of eons of erosion and the force of floodwaters.

Most of us children had been to funerals and knew the rhythm and order, so we tried in childlike ways to mimic them. We chose plots for our small friends with care, laying them to rest next to other past pets we thought they might have liked to play with. The first small coffins were shoe boxes lined with fabric or even wallpaper samples from the big books Father bought at auctions for us girls to use in our homemade dollhouses. By the time we youngest siblings came around, Mother had joined in the rituals and showed us how to line the small boxes with wildflowers—tiny and delicate or more robust, but each plant chosen with care.

In the weeks after a funeral, the grave would cave in as the small cardboard coffins collapsed under the weight of the earth. As with most children's projects, the simply painted names would soon fade. Over time the crosses fell down, brush grew over the sites, and the graves were forgotten by some.

But not by me. I would sit in the grass on the hillside, gaze fixed on the plots for what felt like hours, saddened by the effect of time both on my memory and on the graves themselves. Each animal I got to know on the farm had their own personality quirks; in fact, they weren't that different from people, just less appreciated. Less respected. I felt they needed an advocate or at least someone to mourn them when they were gone. Every creature deserved acknowledgment, I thought, and to not even receive that was the saddest thing I could imagine.

I would often revisit the pets I missed most to talk to them, to make sure they knew I remembered our friendship. I would recite the details of each lost pet and recall our most treasured memories each time I walked between the graves—spoke them repetitively, like a prayer. And then I would smile at the flowers that sprang up over the graves as our beloved pets passed on their life, back into the farm and the forest forever.

That thought made the graveyard a place of quiet comfort for me, and there was something to be said for solitude when growing up with nine siblings and the occasional foster child. Mother had one sibling, and she envied my father his family of sixteen; she wanted the same experience for her children. And so my parents had eleven children—ten surviving—and I was the next to youngest. Mother had so many of us that she eventually stopped going to the hospital to give birth. I like to think that being born on the farm is the reason I've always felt tied to it and to the life residing there.

There is a unique dynamic between children of a large family, one that is hard to understand. My older siblings had a parentlike relationship with us younger kids, but we also recognized the close bonds between siblings near each other in age. We were not merely friends and confidants; we had a built-in drive to protect the younger brother or sister next in line, knowing well how in a large family they could otherwise be overlooked in times of high commotion. This sense of responsibility matured us early, and the bonds it created have stayed with us long after our years on the farm. Yet despite our closeness, when the joyful bustle of a large family became too much, we would seek refuge in the outdoors, either privately or in the company of our nearest sibling.

The solitude of the woods was medicinal for me. I craved these private pilgrimages into the ever-changing forest, and I knew my siblings felt the same way. We each had our secret territories extending to the furthest corners of the eighty-four-acre property. Paul had "Paul's Place" across the road, reached by passing through the swamp, along stone paths and log bridges lined with marsh marigolds and trillium, and all the way down to a secluded pond frequented by great blue herons and turtles. Marla had a cluster of pine trees that formed a sort of teepee, back behind the furthest field. My hideaway was a grove of trees on an island in the middle of a shallow, rocky stream down a horse-made trail from when the loggers came with their Clydesdales and ponies. I enjoyed walking in the cool stream and feeling the pebbles under my feet. It reminded me of a place pixies would surely live.

From an early age, I spent a lot of time freely exploring the woods, with no one wondering where I was—one of the benefits of being a youngest child. But there were dangerous territories that frightened me, and I avoided them when alone. If ever I needed to pass nearby, I felt eyes on me from out of the shadows and made sure I never fully turned my back to them. The little shack constructed of rotting, reused boards and pieces of scrap metal was the perfect hiding place for bears or evil wizards, I thought. The deep swamp between the two back fields was a wonderful place to collect treasures like hundred-year-old bottles, but it was also gloomy and foreboding. The century of farmers before us had dumped discarded equipment alongside the fields they cut out of the forest, and nature had eaten at the piles of antique junk. Trees grew through ancient tractor parts, creating rusty sculptures, half-living, half-metal. Twisted metal and glass became mosaics interspersed with green moss and red leaves. Cow skulls, too, were sprinkled throughout the mud, especially the lower part of the swamp to the left, said to be sinking sand.

Even with my siblings I was cautious in these places, always keeping an eye out for broken bits of spiked fence wire, old traps that trespassing hunters had left, and spots of moss-covered ground that might have concealed hidden streams or sinking sand. Once my shoelaces tangled around barbed wire, and I was terrified I would be stuck there forever—my siblings had already run into the next field and out of sight. I was able to free myself, but only after calming down.

I never quite shook the fear that I would be left behind, left alone. As the baby girl of the family, I often struggled to keep up; and along with my shorter legs and less developed muscles, I had a worsening spinal distortion that made it more and more uncomfortable to run. The sun made me lethargic and lightheaded too, symptoms of a disorder not uncommon to redheads like myself, though I would not receive a diagnosis or explanation for that or my back pain until my teens. But as a child I didn't understand why I fell behind so easily on our farm adventures, and for the eternity of those few panicked minutes alone, I would imagine myself as one of the animals my neighbors trapped in the winter, my foot caught in a snare made tighter by my struggling.

Despite my fears, I found the farm magical, a sanctuary, a place no one else could fully comprehend and that outsiders rarely entered. Butterflies surrounded us, drunk off my mother's acres of beautiful flowers. Every night lightning bugs floated gracefully through the fields like fairies. Matching black-and-white-spotted bunnies and mice littered the landscape, as though the line between domesticated pets and woodland creatures had blurred. Cities of birds communed at the feeders, their songs thankful and like music.

During the evening, after the work was done, Mother—a classically trained pianist—would sit at the piano playing Beethoven or Chopin or an old German folk song passed down from her grandparents, and Father often plugged in a guitar amp as they sang in perfect harmony to an old gospel song or hymn. It was better than any radio station or recording, this symphony of farm and family sounds that combined and changed as you moved around the house and yard: the spring peeper frogs in the background, laughing kids and barking dogs circling outside, the slightly out-of-tune piano from the heart of the house, and my parents and siblings joining in with harmonies and then dropping back to quiet conversation so as not to ruin the effect.

The true magic of the farm was in the land. I vividly remember the sweet, damp scent of the ground as it thawed every spring. Sure, the winter had its own smells: crisp snow and the smoke of the wood burner that heated the farmhouse. But the earth was in our blood, or close to it. There is a theory that microbes in the soil can cause your brain to produce chemicals that make you feel happy and content; my brother Joel told me it ensures farmers return to the land to cultivate it, a way for nature to keep its hold. Perhaps this explains why nothing could replace the sensation of bare feet and hands in the dirt. Even the landmines of thawed dog and cat poop weren't a strong enough deterrent to keep us from reconnecting to the soft spring turf. The land was like another family member that knew everything that had happened there and could understand and comfort like no one else. The farm was in us, and Wolf Creek ran through our veins like blood.

The great melting pot of our farm life was the Amish-built barn, a time-weathered mother personality of warmth, protection, and nourishment. It had existed for a hundred years before we arrived on the farm, and smelled of musty hay and the dust that glimmered in the sunbeams filtering through chinks in the roof and walls. Along the perimeter were pens for larger animals like pigs, chickens, and goats. In smaller pens that Father built, we kept chicks, doves, and rabbits, usually 4-H projects for us kids. Ducks and geese came in and out of the barn at will, depending on the weather.

And the cats! Cats perched everywhere, tending to their mousing duties or lazing about. The hay was a haven for cats, and in the winter the barn would host huge piles of cats wrapped around each other like a quilt of orange, tabby, black, and calico. The cats almost always looked a bit under the weather, with their messy eyes, runny noses, and all-around scraggliness—much like me, their little farm girl counterpart. I even had the constant chapped, runny nose, as if I too had a cold year-round. But healthy or sick, they greeted me with excitement and enthusiastic purring, and every time I walked into the barn, my heart surged at the thought of discovering new life: a tiny kitten or perhaps even a brand-new stray that had found shelter in the hay and was anxious to see a friendly face. My creatures were the perfect remedy anytime I felt down or lonely, and in return I did my best to care for them as pets and friends.

SUPPER TIME

*T*hough food and a feeble attempt at protection were the only gifts I could give my barn cats, I did my very best. My favorite time of day was feeding time. Once I had inherited this chore from my older siblings, I would march out of the kitchen with a bucket full of leftovers and cat food, calling "Heeeeeere, kitty kitty kitty" all the way down to the old milk house entrance of the downstairs barn. Upon the first call, cats from all around the farm, both tame and feral, would scurry to their feet and crowd around me, mewling anxiously as we marched down the driveway. I always felt like I was leading a charge of forty well-trained cat warriors, and I was their proud leader.

Unfortunately our valiant charge often ended in a rout. In the spring, barn swallows would build mud and hay nests in the downstairs barn rafters, low enough that we could climb up on top of old milking stalls to peek inside. Low enough, too, that any human activity nearby was an immediate threat. At feeding time, when the sparrows would see me approaching the barn with my hungry cat horde, they would fly out to protect their barn from the invaders. They'd dive and peck the cats and then me, loudly chirping and circling to bomb us again and again. My eldest brothers taught me to grab handfuls of gravel from the driveway and throw the stones high into the air. This worked well until a stray rock would hit me on the head on the way down, and at that point I'd bolt for the safety of the barn, my army of cats at my heels.

Inside the barn I would pour the food evenly into large saucer pans that had been retired from the kitchen. The loud, meowing crowd would rush around the perimeters of the pans, but I made sure the small and shy cats had room at the supper table too. Inevitably they would be pushed aside again by a more aggressive cat, so I would hurry to reshift cats around. It got to be a pattern after a while. I quickly learned each cat's personality and figured out how to keep the balance; if a greedy cat started to growl or hiss, I would scold them and move them to their own pan away from the others, all the while explaining how such a poor attitude would only set them back. My lesson was usually responded to with an angry side glance or a grumble from a mouth half-full of food.

I always placed a pan farther away for the wildest cats that were too anxious to come closer. They lurked a good ten feet away from the rest, licking their lips—and I knew they must be hungry, since they were skinnier than the rest of the bunch. Though my distribution of the dinner meat always started with the sickest-looking cats, I'd give it next as a peace offering to the feral cats, hoping to charm them into becoming my friends. It never worked. They snatched the meat from me, hissing, dragging it somewhere private to enjoy, and perhaps reveling in their ability to steal the farmer's precious chicken so easily!

Though I prepared warm, comfortable places in the barn for the cats to stay, they preferred standing ready by the front and kitchen doors to dash into the house the second anyone entered or exited. A few cats were particularly clever; they ran for the upstairs and hid, waiting for an opportunity to slink down later, when they'd be less expected. Surprisingly, even the untamed cats knew to do this. But most sprinted directly toward the kitchen, jumping across tables, counters, and the stove top and grabbing for pieces of meat.

I marveled at how every cat was born knowing the location of that kitchen, which was always full of food. Mother would cook enough to feed an army and set it out for us on the counter before dawn. The food sat out all day so that everyone could eat at will, but Mother would declare, "That's how the pioneers did it," and sure enough, none of us ever suffered food poisoning.

The cats didn't seem to mind either; sometimes as many as six or seven of them would hang by their claws from the screen door, insisting on being let in. When the cat chorus became too loud and the wooden screen door rattled from all the commotion, one of my brothers would usually fill a pitcher of water to throw through the screen to clear them off. I would run to unhook as many kitties as I could reach, but for every one I took off the screen, another climbed up, and I knew it was only a matter of time before I was drying off my poor cats and scowling at my brothers.

It was protocol that every time one of us left the house, we had to open the screen as fast as possible, grabbing handfuls of the cats trying to dart inside—an all-in-one scooping and tossing and closing. I remember Father and Rachel scurrying around with brooms, shooing out the cats that had slipped through our defenses. But I knew that outside the cats had to contend with harsh weather, predators, and cars, and it was difficult not to give into their constant pleading to be let indoors. During the cold winters I often tried to buy the kitties some time inside the house, which only reinforced their behavior, but they were always shown the door before long.

Despite my efforts, our small family farm was a fragile bubble carved into the unrelenting forest along a wild creek. Most animals here lived a short life, whether by design or by accident. I knew we had to guard our hearts when getting close to farm cats; we could love deeply but with an understanding that our time might be limited. They roamed, got hurt more often, and sometimes just disappeared. I also knew that as farmers, our priority was survival, and this meant protecting the animals that fed us: the cows, the pigs, the chickens. All others took a lower priority. But my heart could never understand that cold approach. When I found helpless fur balls mewing blindly, mistaking me for their mother, I happily risked losing my heart to a tiny life in need of me. And so the bond between us instilled in me a responsibility for their wellbeing, lasting the duration of their life.

ORANGIE

As far back as I have memory, I have believed it was my sacred responsibility to advocate for all farm cats, but I always had a few favorites. I, of all people, understood the need for some creatures to feel special when they were lost in a horde of other creatures—or in my case, other siblings. I had a whole system for lavishing attention on the cats most in need of it, complete with favorite cats for different kids, and special days, like made-up birthdays and anniversaries, for cats and stuffed animals alike.

Then there were the personal favorites, the ones I considered almost part of the family. The first favorite I remember was named Orangie—an unimaginative name, I know, but not a horrible naming job for a five-year-old, which is how old I was at the time. I regularly chose orange kittens as my declared favorites because I had empathy for them; they always seemed, in my eyes, anyway, sicklier than the rest. I believed I was a sickly redhead too, with my pale skin and more health issues than the rest of my siblings combined. Besides a severely curved spine, spina bifida, and the thin membrane disease that made me dizzy in the hot farm sun, I had constant ear infections so bad that blood dripped from my ears and stained my pillows at night. Later the ear infections led to hearing loss, resulting in a speech impediment. I can confirm from old photos that I was a mess to look at: an eternally red chapped spot above my lip, hand-me-down clothing from my four older sisters, and my hair in a bright, fiery red mess, not too different from the scraggly orange fur of my kitten lookalikes. I needed them; they needed me. So the orange kitties and I stuck together.

I remember dragging Orangie everywhere during the day and sneaking out to the porch in my pajamas at night to visit him. He would cry at the back porch door, hoping I would take pity on him and shower him with attention—which of course I did. How I hated having to leave him behind in the cold night! He learned to expect my visits and would hang by his claws on the screen door, calling for me long after I climbed into bed. His sad cry broke my heart every time. I eagerly listened for the sound to stop but never dared sneak him indoors, since the porch door was next to my parents' bedroom and my mother had the hearing of a bat.

Orangie grew into an adult cat—too heavy to carry, so he followed me everywhere instead. Yet I don't recall seeing him padding after me the afternoon Marla and I were playing on the tractor wagon by the upstairs barn. The old wooden wagon had one set of wheels in the center and a long metal neck at the front, and that day Marla and I were running along the top of the wagon from one side to the other, making the neck go up and down like a seesaw. This was the closest thing we had to a playground, other than the giant sandbox my father had built that inevitably had become the farm's largest litter box. Of course the wagon wasn't particularly safe, so Rachel appeared long enough to warn us not to play on farm equipment, then went back to reading her book.

Rachel was always a sensible girl, and reminded me of the strict schoolteachers from the stories we read. In fact, like most of my older siblings, she did eventually become a teacher. She often scolded us, but sometimes she gathered us all around her at night to read us novels about kingdoms of noble animals living in the woods. We would huddle close behind her when there were pictures, but when there were none, we would lie back on the beds and listen.

Back then just we youngest three girls shared a room, Marla and I in one bed and Rachel in her own on the neat side of the room. Her bed was always perfectly made, complete with a well-placed embroidered pillow that I think she made herself. Rachel forbade us even to touch her bed, which made it all the more irresistible. Once when she left for school, Marla and I gave in to temptation and took a running leap up onto Rachel's bed, jumping higher and higher, our hearts racing with the excitement of our rebellion. And then one of my baby teeth fell out. Marla and I searched frantically for that tooth, as it was evidence of the trespassing, but we never did find it. Fortunately, neither did Rachel.

Rachel could usually strike enough fear in our hearts to get us to do what she said. Just not this time in regard to the tractor wagon.

Marla and I liked to run back and forth on the wagon because every time its metal neck clanked loudly into the earth, the boards shook and our footing became unsteady. Whoever was able to stay on the wagon the longest without falling was the winner. But this day we had only just begun playing on our makeshift seesaw when Orangie caught up like a good best friend. Like a bad friend, I didn't even see him arrive. Right away he found himself between the metal wagon shaft and the dirt, and the moment the wagon post landed flat on his neck, he began spinning around, screaming and bleeding. The tormented cat screams will always haunt my memory and my consciousness. But I didn't stay to see the end.

Terrified, Marla and I ran sobbing for the house, that short stretch across the yard and driveway seeming like an eternity. I scarcely registered the sharpness of the driveway gravel under my bare feet. My memory cuts out as we struggled to open the front door, but somehow we ended up in the bathtub, still sobbing as Mother told us gently that our father had "taken care" of Orangie and buried him in a peaceful place under a tree. For days after that I tried to gather the courage to ask Father to show me Orangie's grave, but I never did. I was too ashamed and brokenhearted to face it. I still thought of Orangie when I passed through the graveyard, though, whether or not he was buried there. That was my place set aside to reflect on all my lost animals.

I never got over the death of Orangie. Like Mother said, accidents happened, but that was the first time a creature under my care had met their demise through my fault. The brutality of the gentle cat's death fed my fears but also my determination: I would never allow another careless, needless death, not under my watch and certainly not because of me. And so the struggle began between helping and harming, a delicate balance that I could never quite master back then.

I didn't want to be the sickly orange kitten; I longed to be strong and brave. I tried not to show anyone my fears and vulnerabilities. I did not decorate my bedroom with princesses or pink and purple but with leopards and lions. I was an untamed wildcat too, I thought: capable and fierce, a courageous lion with a bright-red mane. I suppose I was tired of being the runt of the family, both in size and in health. Or maybe I just didn't like feeling helpless, unable to protect the creatures I loved.

Sometime after Orangie's death, I became obsessed with wildcats. I loved the way they stood out from the average domestic cat, the way I wished I could among my siblings. The idea of acquiring kinship with such an animal sounded like a true feat of bravery, and I thought they might be able to protect the rest of the animals on the farm from predators, though they were predators themselves.

I had read that the large cats preferred to sleep in rocky, cavelike areas, so I started sneaking to a spot in the woods on our neighbor's property, where towering hemlock trees rose out of boulders sprinkled with pine needles, moss, and ferns. Above the rocky incline was a ledge where a huge pine had grown, its roots spread over the boulders like pythons, and I could stand on the edge of this cliff and survey the valley right down to where the stream below trickled through the spongy ground at the base. I suspected there were bobcats in our valley—my siblings had heard their screams—and though I knew this was a stretch and that the plan was severely flawed, I kept hoping to discover a baby bobcat tragically separated from its mother. Finally, after many failed expeditions, I casually asked Mother if she had seen baby bobcats in the woods.

I suspect she was on to my plan, because instead of answering my question, she explained to me that feeding such an animal would cost a fortune in milk. She must also have tipped off my father, who bought me a 1950s children's book titled something like *Little Leopards Become Big Leopards and Big Leopards Kill*. The story goes as you would expect: a friendly orphaned leopard kitten grows to adulthood and has his first taste of blood after compassionately licking a toddler's scraped knee. Then, of course, he becomes feral and kills the entire village. I had to admit that maybe a wildcat would not do after all. Instead I decided to reform as many would-be wilder cats, the smaller variety living in our barn, as I could.

WILD ONES

But there was a thin line even between the feral and the tame cats. Both worked so hard to survive, hunting their own food—a wonderful service to our family—and weathering the worst of nature with only a little help from our barn.

What I wouldn't have done to see the wilder cats run around the farm carefree with the rest of the cats, purring for a petting! Instead they hid and hissed and sometimes clawed at us in fear. They were mysteries to me, their lives stories I wished I knew. Were they once tame? Did they have a home long ago but were now driven mad by loneliness and the desperation to survive our deep Pennsylvania woods? They seemed so unhappy and ill, and this weighed heavily on my heart.

There wasn't any way to tame cats after they had grown out of the kitten stage, which meant that if I wanted to protect them, I needed to start right after their birth. I devoted much effort to finding new litters before it was too late and the kittens joined the feral population of the farm.

There was an art to catching barn kittens. My sisters and I would creep around the stored furniture in our cluttered old barn and climb up into the rafters and flimsy lofts to listen for kitten action: claws scratching on cardboard or tiny, muffled mews. Then all we had to do was uncover the nest of kittens. They might be in an old dresser drawer or a forgotten cardboard box or under a pile of crates, cuddling in the dark. It was like finding treasure—furry, adorable treasure. I loved lying on the barn floor, using my body like a fence so I could watch them play and learn as I introduced them to a world bigger than their nest.

The key to catching the slightly older, wilder kittens was to sneak up very slowly with small, controlled motions. Even if the kitten saw us, they wouldn't know what they were looking at if they'd never seen a human before, so they wouldn't be alarmed so long as we were careful not to startle them. Sometimes it took us as much as twenty minutes, only moving when the kitten was turned away and then freezing as soon as they looked back. When I was finally just a couple of feet away, leaning over top of the kitten, they would grow suspicious, and that's when I had to act fast, lunging to catch them under the arms or by the scruff of the neck. Sometimes I'd miss, and then they were all the harder to catch the next time around, having become a little more world-wise. What's more, they might fight back—but I didn't give up, even when they clawed at my hands till I bled or they sank their little teeth into my skin. I knew this was their only chance, the moment that determined tame cat or feral. For me, it was just a few scratches. For them, it could be a matter of life and death.

Mother and Father repeatedly tried to instill a practical, farmer's maturity in us: we couldn't fight nature, and cats in the wild simply wouldn't survive. But my parents also raised me with a Christian heart, to help others in need, and I noticed them helping anyone they met, no matter the circumstances or how rough the person seemed. Mother could care for countless children, whether they were hers or in foster care, and with equal passion could nurse a sick animal or transplant a simple root to build a full garden. I believe this compassion also burned in my hands and in my heart.

I would often pity the barn cats too, because they did not live the spoiled life of indoor pets. They seemed happy, though, in their community, and there was no shortage of fresh milk, table scraps, and warm hay for them to enjoy. In fact, many house cats I meet these days don't seem as affectionate or as easily amused as the farm cats I was raised with. I always figure that farm cats just know they're lucky and don't take anything for granted.

GIVER OF LIFE

The way I have always summed up my mother is that she is one with nature. When I was growing up, Mother never spent a second on her appearance; she didn't wear jewelry or makeup, didn't buy colorful clothing. But she was beautiful in the most natural sense, and never more beautiful than when she was covered in earth from gardening. No one ever made mud look so elegant.

The woods surrounding the farmhouse were filled with endless clusters of wildflowers, and Mother found the colors and patterns so full of wonder that she wanted to bring this exotic beauty closer to home. Planting and harvesting became a source of peace for her, and also for anyone who enjoyed her bouquets. Mother, Paul, and Joel all took great joy in arranging bouquets to decorate the house and deliver to the local hospital or to shut-ins and people with permanent disabilities.

I have fond memories of expeditions into the swamps to dig up wildflowers. Our mother would dress us in secondhand clothes and our oldest mud shoes and hand small trowels to the smaller children, larger shovels to the older kids, and empty buckets to everyone. We would pass through the orchard, skirting the graveyard, and follow the creek as it meandered through the muddy swampland. Occasionally we would stray from our path, led on by all manner of blossoming discoveries. The bogs were interspersed with hemlocks on mossy islands dotted with violets and Dutchman's-breeches. Little white pantaloon-shaped flow-

SICK KITTENS

I fought against my kittens' illnesses with all the determination of a child who can't or won't accept the reality of nature. When kittens are very small, fleas can make them anemic and weak, so Mother and I would regularly team up at the kitchen sink to wash them and apply flea powder. Kittens could also get colds so bad that their eyes would completely seal over with hard goo. Most of the barn kittens we caught developed this to some degree, and since some had eyes that were stuck closed, they weren't too hard to sneak up on to help. Mother and I would wash the infected eyes with warm water until they opened up and we could treat them with medicine. We did this every day, because if a kitten's eyes were sealed up for too long, they would become blind. In nature that is a tragedy; a blind cat is an almost-dead cat, since it is almost impossible for them to avoid predatory animals and even cars. Most of the kittens with vision issues simply disappeared before adulthood—one more reason to keep an ear out for meows from new litters in the barn and rescue the kittens before it was too late.

The most common killer of small kittens on the farm was mange, a nasty skin disease that compromised the immune systems of weaker cats. Their fur would fall out, their skin would break out in scabs and sores, and they might lose weight and become dehydrated, leaving them susceptible to other illnesses or to predators. I nursed these kittens around the clock, washing them, applying medicine, and even force-feeding them with tiny baby bottles made for their small mouths. These were living baby dolls, not like the ones other kids got from the store, and as they struggled to drink the raw milk mixed with egg yolk and medicine, I felt like they truly needed me. Sometimes, though, I was just making them more miserable up to the point when they became too tired to fight it and died in my arms. I remember them crying like babies through the night, their constant mews weaving in and out of my troubled dreams.

Even among the older cats, sickness spread easily. When one of our pets fell ill, we knew their chances of survival were slim. Some diseases were so severe and so fast-acting that it wasn't unheard of to discover ten or twenty dead cats on the barn floor before we even knew they weren't feeling well. Kittens and elderly cats died first, usually within twenty-four hours. The others lay around depressed and lethargic, or worse, biting at their back legs and tails, causing infections that swamped their already compromised immune systems. I did my best to help the barn cats, but no matter how sick the feral cats were, their terror of us gave them just enough energy to flee my help and hide somewhere out of reach. They usually died in the woods or tucked away in a secret place. I hated that some cats had to be feral; my heart broke for them. Instead of helping them, I made their deaths colder, lonelier, and scary.

Lessons like this instill a certain stubbornness that never goes away. Do you let pain stop the caring? Do you allow the harsh reality of death to end your fight for life? These are heavy weights for a kid, but to me it was always worth it to help creatures in their hour of greatest need, even if it led to heartache on my part. I had to believe that at least being present meant something, so that they would not be alone at the end.

Nothing comforted me more than watching a once-suffering cat return to playing happily in the farm- yard. I considered those cats miracles, and for a while the miracle kitty would get special attention, like extra scraps, cuddles, and the right to live in the house if it was a particu- larly incredible recovery. The hope of healing was always worth the risk of heartbreak. And so I continued pouring myself into them. I continued to make my heart vulnerable. And I tried to extend my protection to other helpless crea- tures, hoping that they too could feel a measure of comfort and safety amid the harshness of life in the wild.

HEART ATTACK BUNNIES

*E*ven as we defended our animals against larger threats, I also tried to protect the farm's smaller creatures from the cats I considered my friends. Our tamer house and barn cats would bring their half-dead catches to the front door of the house to play with and, I suspect, to show them off to us. On many occasions I would walk out the kitchen door and find a dead mouse, chipmunk, or bird—an offering of thanks for all the care we gave, or maybe the suggestion of a much-needed ingredient in that night's meal. For a while I could never figure out which cat kept leaving one single organ on the steps. Was it a greedy cat devouring the best of the offering? Or did the cat think they were giving up the most important part of the creature, where they thought the victim's soul resided? Each little gift always left much speculation. But I was far from proud or grateful, as the cats might have hoped. I was mortified, ashamed of their cruelty.

My cats often joined me on my solitary quests into the woods, but sometimes they used the excursion as an opportunity to stalk prey startled by my passing. It bothered me that my otherwise sweet companions would happily destroy whatever they caught. Sometimes I would save the cricket or bird, and sometimes I just had to let it be. It was a strange thing to figure out so young: when to intervene and when to decide it was best or perhaps even necessary to let nature take its course. I leaned more toward saving everything I could, but I also watched and learned from my older siblings and listened to their counsel on the importance of the food chain, the practical realities of farm life, or their own sad experiences. Still, I imagined a world where it all worked together, and I did my best to make it so.

I remember the first baby bunny I tried to save. Bunnies were the most fainthearted animals that wandered the farm, and they were very popular—loved by foxes, coyotes, dogs, and even my own cats. They weren't hard to find in the woods if I kept an eye out for little brown fur balls under shrubs or piles of leaves. Sometimes my heart would jump at the sight of a hidden bit of rabbit fur, and I would swoop it up, only to realize it was just a bit of rabbit fluff left behind by a cat or other woodland predator. That happened quite a bit, as the bunnies' instinct was to freeze instead of run when approached by a predator. I figured that was why rabbits had to have so many babies, because this particular defense didn't seem to work very well.

One evening I was on dish drying duty, and my siblings and I were singing along to tapes, when I heard sudden screaming out in the yard. Dropping my towel into the sink, I ran outside onto the lawn to find a helpless baby bunny trapped tight in a barn cat's jaw. I grabbed the cat and pried his mouth open with both hands, cutting up my fingers on his teeth, though I barely felt it then. I knew exactly how to maneuver his jaw to ensure no more harm came to the victim, because the same situation had happened with my gerbil Murry. I could feel the strength in my arms as adrenaline pumped through me. I knew I would never give up, no matter the biting and the clawing.

As soon as the bunny fell out of the cat's mouth, I dashed to grab him to safety. But by then we had an audience of other barn cats and even a few feral cats that had found the courage to approach when they heard the frightened rabbit and recognized the chance for a free meal. I had to act fast, running alongside the cats, prying the bunny out of yet another mouth or two before I won. I picked up the bleeding ball of fluff, holding him close. His little black eyes bulged with shock, and I could feel his heart pounding on my hand. I'd seen other rescued baby rabbits drop dead of a heart attack, but this one just sat frozen in terror, so I held him on my lap and tried to comfort him. Fantasies flooded my mind: the baby rabbit growing used to me and becoming my pet. When he seemed calmer, I prepared a comfortable box for him to live in and set him against a sunny window.

But he refused even to eat the lettuce I brought him. He just sat frozen, looking terrified, and eventually he died from his wounds.

None of that stopped me from intervening on behalf of bunnies again, and field mice, even moles, making homes for them in shoe boxes filled with my gerbils' bedding, nuts, lettuce, and a mayo lid for water. I rescued chipmunks in a similar way, especially those that were too injured to run after being dropped at my feet by proud cats. I held them for hours, admittedly enjoying the chance for closeness with critters that were usually too wild to dote on. This was one of my biggest vices. Deep down I think I knew that holding them would cause more distress, but sometimes I was too excited to leave them be. Perhaps I also needed to believe I could bring them some comfort after what they had been through thanks to my pets.

Unlike the bunnies, many of these little rodents survived, and I eventually released them into the woods, leaving them an overturned tissue box as a temporary home filled with fluff and snacks. I kept hoping they would come back to live there as my half-tame, half-wild pets. But they never did.

POSSUM

I had a soft spot for many of the other woodland creatures, even the uglier variety. I was particularly fascinated with opossums, probably because they were
relatively gentle creatures and got a bad rap. I suppose
I pitied them. Once in a while I would see them running
across the road with their babies hurrying along behind,

and I couldn't help following them, though their fuzzy, coarse hair and wormlike tails made it hard to imagine snuggling them. They always seemed to have that fake smile too, the kind people sometimes give—"I'm smiling to make you feel better, but really I don't care." That made me want their attention all the more.

The opossums were usually too nervous to come close to the house, but they snacked at the large compost pile we kept at the edge of the field. That was where we dumped our slops after meals so it could turn into fertilizer for the gardens. I often tried to sneak up on the opossums for a closer look, but they were easy to startle and would either waddle away awkwardly when they saw me or would flop over to play dead. At first I would fall for it, assuming the poor creature had been killed by one of the dogs, but then I would realize shortly afterward that the opossum had gotten up and hustled away after I'd turned my back. When I caught on to this trick, I found it endearing. Out of courtesy, and so as not to upset the ridiculous creatures, I would always pretend to be fooled by their trick and would walk away loudly so they'd know it was safe to move again.

In one instance of particularly bad timing, a mother opossum did not hear me coming, and that created a predicament. I had stepped into the downstairs barn to feed the chickens and found myself three feet from the startled mother and her six newborn babies riding on her back. She looked terrified, like she knew it was too late to play dead, so I slowly moved backward toward the door. But then she bolted deeper into the barn. In her rush to escape, every one of her tiny babies fell off her back and onto the cold cement floor.

My mind whirled. The babies were so young that they were still naked of fur and too small and weak to get around on their own. I couldn't just leave them for the mother to retrieve—a cat would be around momentarily and would no doubt gobble up every last one. But I knew the mother wouldn't want my scent on her babies, so I waited outside the barn, just out of view but close enough to guard the entrance from cats. I kept peeking over the lower half of the barn door to see if the mother had returned. She didn't come back. I wanted to wait longer, but the babies did not look well, and when the weather took an even colder turn, I felt I had no choice. I picked them up and placed them on a warm dish towel, then brought them somewhere safe where I could feed them kitten formula with a dropper. I knew that even if my rescue efforts worked, I would not be allowed to raise the baby opossums; I just wanted to keep them alive long enough to return them to their mother. I wondered where the mother was and how upset she must be. Yet I did not see her in the barn or anywhere, and I realized she must have left the barn through another exit.

Each of the babies died that evening, and my heart broke. I wondered if I should bring them back to the barn so that the mother would know and stop looking for them. But I did not want them to become a meal for a cat, dog, or raccoon. Eventually I placed their dish towel bed in a shoe box, tucked another cloth over top of their cold bodies, and buried them on the graveyard slope. They were the only opossums to get an honorable burial there.

"FREE KITTENS"

As time passed I opened my heart to still more animals, particularly the unwanted and often sick drop-offs that ended up on our farm from time to time. It wasn't uncommon for a town family, when faced with a pet's terminal illness, to decide that a nice, quiet retirement to a farm in the country could be a good solution and perhaps an exciting new home for their pet ...fresh air and other cats and dogs to play with, of course. Kids at school would refer to their pets "going to live on the farm," and I knew that sometimes it was a lie parents told to cover up a beloved pet's death, but often it was nothing more than a quick drop-off and getaway at the entrance to our long driveway. "Farmers can always use more cats to catch mice," some said. I used to wonder why no one understood we didn't have the money to care for these pets, but now I suppose it was a way people relieved themselves of both a problem and any associated guilt. Still, regardless of their origin or their health, I welcomed these "problems" with great enthusiasm and did what I could to make them feel at home.

And we certainly weren't innocent of relocating cats ourselves. When we younger kids were distracted, Mother and Father did sneak some cats off to the apple orchard miles away, particularly during financially tight times when we couldn't afford the massive amounts of cat food they needed. I suppose in our situation my parents were re-dropping off those poor cats. Or at least buying time until they inevitably found their way back to us.

Adoption was a different matter, and we had to keep close inventory of our kitties. Nursing them back to health was just half the battle; in the greatest of ironies, the kittens we played with the most became the friendliest and therefore the most prized for adoption. In the end, by rescuing them we were only making them trusting enough for adults to gather into cars and take to a new home far away.

It seemed as though no matter how many dozens of cats we had, the one that Mother was sending home with another kid was the one we could not possibly live without. Sometimes I would be working at the family farm market when Mother would haul in a huge cage lined with old towels and proudly display our cutest kittens at the front of the stall. Of course I usually saw it coming; for weeks I would plead that the kittens were too young (even when I knew they were not) or strike bargains and then change the terms of the bargain, like which kitten I wanted to keep most, every day. Marla, on the other hand, was the loudest when cousins or strangers were about to take home one of our treasured kittens. She would squeal, "But that one's my favorite!" and retreat behind the house to cry while the new owners drove off with our kitties. Occasionally Mother would give in to our tears when she knew we were particularly close to a kitten. But other times they were simply gone before we even knew their leaving was an option.

One unforgettable day I came home from elementary school and discovered that most of my cats had vanished. In a panic, I asked my brothers and sisters, then Mother, who I remember avoided the subject in some adult manner—her parental scolding indicative of her guilt. I finally figured out that Father had rehomed most of the cats to thin our ever-increasing herd. The justification was that we'd had more than we could afford to feed, but I had never been so horrified in all my childhood—most of my best friends in the world had been ripped from me without my having the chance to say good-bye. And the reason they were picked was that I had taught them to be so trusting of humans. They were the first to come when called, and so they were the ones taken.

At the farm market, Mother would put a "Free Kittens" sign on the front of the cage, and sure enough, every young child wandering through the aisles of produce and flowers would spot the meowing balls of fur and throw fits until their mother either agreed to take one home or dragged the child away kicking and screaming. I remember listening anxiously while I swept the aisles, praying that the mother would resist her bratty child's pleas and leave the kittens behind for us. Worse was when the kittens accompanied Mother to the farm market, but I did not. On days I wasn't working, I waited at the top of the driveway at a quarter to ten, after the shop closed, anxiously counting little heads in the dark as Mother approached.

Sometimes it turned out well in the end—for us kids, at least. Occasionally cats and dogs that had been adopted would walk the miles back home again, and sometimes cousins and farm market customers returned kittens outright. Then we would celebrate their return, showering them with love and a few extra treats for what we'd put them through. But this did not mean they wouldn't be stolen away again.

Even my stuffed animals were not safe. A lot of my favorite toys were hand-me-downs and not in the best shape. After catching my mother throwing away the dirtiest of my old bears, I became regimented in my care, constantly washing my stuffed animals in the sink and then hanging them on the line to dry outside. Oftentimes Blue-y, my old blue bear, wasn't even completely dry before I began washing him again, keeping a distrusting eye on my mother the whole time. Ironically, because of the overwashing, the cotton in Blue-y's belly became full of mold and mildew, or at least that's what his smell began to suggest. But I think Mother got the message loud and clear that he was off bounds.

THE PROFESSOR

I f Mother was my clear ally in my quest to protect the smaller farm animals, Father was a little more difficult to figure out. My father was a professor of mathematics and physics, a civil defense officer specializing in radiological defense, a begrudging exorcist, a UFO investigator, and an ordained pastor, and was considered a local genius—but he was not particularly knowledgeable in the ways of affection or tenderness. He was much like his own father, who from what I understand was a sort of mad professor in his town. Though my grandparents were long gone before I had the opportunity to meet them, I heard all about Grandpa Voltz like he was Nikola Tesla himself. Father recounted stories of how Grandpa had wired his mother's house for electricity before the age of ten, and as an adult had built the first electric furnace and a Cherry Picker but had passed up the opportunity to patent them. Grandpa had started college at MIT, but when the financing fell through early on, he dropped out of school and continued his education on his own through books and experiments. He had a room full of homemade electronics, and his bedroom sported an entire wall of ham radio equipment that he'd built from World War II surplus parts. There were first-generation electric car parts and atom smasher pieces in the barn, and behind that a backyard full of telephone poles with wires strung between them like giant antennae.

My favorite story about my grandfather was of the seven-foot robot he built in the 1950s—our "Uncle Clarence"—who ran on wheels through the house and answered the front door with a prerecorded greeting when salesmen or one of the eight daughters' terrified dates came to call. I only had the chance to see Clarence once, long after he had been deactivated. I looked into his dark eyes, wondering what stories he could tell about Grandpa, who was all fantastic tales and myths to me.

Grandpa Voltz's last job was working with an atom smasher at a nuclear research center that handled uranium products. He and many of his colleagues eventually experienced blood clots and overall poor health, dying relatively young. Though it was never confirmed whether this had anything to do with their exposure to radiation, I sometimes wondered if this was what had turned Father into a bit of a conspiracy theorist. Though I suppose radiation exposure due to wild experiments in energy was an honorable demise for an eccentric scientist with the name of Voltz.

Father would do farm work in old dress pants and suspenders—always the dignified, learned professor, even out in the field. When he wasn't grading papers or doing chores, he was reading in his comfortable old leather armchair, which was patched up with duct tape—one of the best tools, he always said. And every night he read from his old Bible, which was so worn out that the cover was held together by duct tape, of course. I once took him in to elementary school for show-and-tell as a "record-breaking speed reader" so that he could demonstrate in front of the class. The show was complete with a quiz afterward, which he aced.

Father was on a never-ending, all-encompassing quest for truth. He wanted to know how we know what we think we know, and questioned everything. And in that chair he studied alternative historical and scientific theories not taught in schools, reading books on strange phenomena like giants or UFOs and controversial religious writings like the Apocrypha and the Book of Enoch. When welcoming new students at the beginning of the semester, he handed out color-coded papers on topics such as how to survive a nuclear blast and how to perform an exorcism— topics he believed were more important and even more useful than those you'd get in a typical textbook. In fact, it was not unusual to hear Father performing an exorcism on a stranger in the living room while we kids sat at the dining room table, playing cards like it was a completely normal evening. Unconventional interests for a farmer, to be sure.

But Father was no ordinary man.

Father was a mathematician in every way; to him, life was an equation of scripture and discipline. And while there were no outright verbal expressions of love for us, there was no direct negativity either. We had no fighting in our house. No yelling. Not between our parents and not between us. There was respect and order, and Father was the head of the household, honored and feared to a healthy degree.

But I remember a few times cracks appeared in his severe demeanor. Sometimes as we tiptoed past Father reading in his chair, careful not to disturb him, he would quickly snap a hand around one of our small feet without even glancing up from his book, and then he'd start tickling. We'd fall over giggling to the point of tears and then sneak by over and over, hoping he would break away from his reading to do it again.

It was hard to slip anything past Father, even when he was wrapped up in his studies. He always knew when cats had sneaked into the house to jump onto the kitchen counter—or worse, make themselves comfortable on his bed. He seemed to hate cats generally, and I suspected he didn't see much point in their existence beyond their catching mice. Though he never said it aloud, I knew he wasn't happy that my mother and I kept promoting particular barn cats to house cat status, but since he would never actually argue with Mother, he resorted to wearing a pin with a crossed-out cat on the front. This was his silent protest.

One of our black-and-white cats didn't seem to take the hint. She grew attached to Father for some unknown reason and enjoyed sleeping as close as she could get away with when he was reading in his chair in the living room. Of course she never made it all the way to his lap, but she certainly tested her limits. All of us kids, of course, got a huge kick out of watching this effort—"Does he see her yet? Wait till he sees her!"—and would collapse with laughter when Father finally slammed down his book and waved his arms in the air, yelling, "Get away, cat!" They were all just "cat" to him.

Later in life I learned, to my shock, that Father actually liked cats. Apparently he enjoyed putting on the grouchy man show for us, and our reaction gave him just as much entertainment as his did for us. I also discovered years later that he was terribly allergic, and that the cats he let us have in the house caused him much respiratory distress. Yet he let it slide because he saw the joy it brought to us kids and to Mother.

THE WORLD OUTSIDE

*B*oth my father and mother were stoic and hardworking—an epic pioneer team that not only supported a career and a farm, but also raised a vast collection of children and other lost souls, human and animal alike. Not surprisingly, there wasn't much time for us individually, and we had to respect that. But we were close as a group, and finding my place in the midst of the family taught me how to rely on myself, turning me to the comforting presence of the woods and the warmth of furry creatures to help me process my fears.

And there were many. As a child I was ruled by fear, and when I let my imagination run wild, it controlled me. Just like any kid, I was afraid of the dark and of getting lost in the grocery store, but I had a whole other layer of fears that set me apart from others my age: UFOs, demons, the government, the apocalypse, and the rapture, all topics my father discussed in great depth.

I remember hearing that my father was a target because of his conspiracy theories and nonconventional knowledge. He showed us an escape path in the woods should anyone dangerous come to the farm for him or Mother. I imagined the horror of the world outside that would send such people in, and in my head the farm became the only safe place on earth—and leaving it was the stuff of my nightmares.

Every time one of my parents left the farm without me, I felt in my heart that it would be the last time I saw them. I vividly remember the evening they wrote their will in the dining room while we kids bustled around getting ready for bed. They delegated each younger child to a married older sibling's family, and I was assigned to Ray and his wife, Jane. A desperate loneliness flooded my heart as I imagined being sent far away to live with my oldest brother, never to see the farm again. I burst into tears then, and when Mother asked, "What is wrong, Elisabeth?" I declared, "I don't want you to die!" It was perhaps the only outburst I ever made in front of my parents, which embarrassed me greatly. Mother looked down at my sobbing figure, smiled gently, and tried to explain that a will was a precaution that parents of all ages took. Then she poured a bath for me, which felt like a warm hug, as always—her way of comforting me. I sat in the bath wondering how long I would have with my dear parents, who were as old as some of my classmates' grandparents, and whatever would happen to all our pets if we had to leave the farm. Surely Ray and Jane wouldn't let me bring any of them with me to the suburbs. It was a real dilemma.

I was baffled when my classmates described their greatest stresses, like arguments with their parents over how many sweets they were permitted to have. I couldn't wrap my head around a life where these would be a kid's

biggest worries. Even their casual conversations were con-
fusing to me, and a huge bore—didn't they know there were
greater concerns in life than the silly topics they gossiped
about? At recess I found myself running alongside the boys,
a more fitting place for a tomboy who'd grown up on the
farm, but with all the asphalt and so few creatures, it too
felt like an alien outdoor world. I became private, guarded,
and drew closer to animals than to other children my age,
who I was convinced couldn't understand my concerns or
the way of life of a large family on a farm such as ours.

The outside world was a bit of a mystery to me,
but the farm seemed a beautiful safe haven, and I fully em-
braced my role in this sanctuary. There I was the wood elf,
running full speed through the forest barefoot, rolling my
feet over branches and leaves so carefully as I sensed them
that I made very little sound. I took pride in being able to
hide behind brush and high up in pine trees when nervous
city cousins came to visit, intruders in our sacred, private
woods. I knew it was a good day when I was really dirty.
Dust from the hayloft, clay and mud from the creek, soil
from the gardens. Grease from bikes and machinery. Green-
stained feet from the grass, and rough hands from the dirt,

and of course sweat from hard work and play. Perhaps the smell of a cat or dog that had chosen to roll in something pungent. The essence of the farm fed my soul, and I believed it could do the same for the creatures that arrived there, seeking sanctuary.

It was no wonder I became the keeper of the most helpless of the small animals, for better or for worse: Creatures the outside world had failed and castoffs that had been dumped out of cars next to the willow tree at our farm entrance, unwanted, flawed, even dying. Hungry, ragged cats and dogs that climbed out of the woods and made a new home in our barn. Helpless baby animals of all kinds that suddenly appeared out of the barn every season. Seeing what life could do to these poor creatures added to my cynicism. The world outside seemed so unloving, so mysterious—I wanted nothing more than to gather my multitude of pets and tell them they were safe under my watch and in my barn. This sense of responsibility became my drive. But that meant it also became my fault when these creatures suffered.

JACK

Ducks had a special place in my heart too, and also on my lap. Maybe it was because of their ridiculous appearance, with their big, silly feet and bills, and the way they huddled together, quacking under their breath like a bunch of petty gossips. They always seemed like such judgmental, catty lots, but I loved them for all their attitude.

And perhaps for their extremely huggable shape—much less slippery than sleek cats, which would wriggle out of my arms the moment I caught them. I had a knack for catching ducks in their pen or in the yard, and when I wrapped my arms snug around their torsos in just the right way, their wings were pinned back so they could not struggle while I showered them with love. It was pretty easy to pretend they liked it—I suspect, at least, that they enjoyed the attention.

My first ducks were a gift from Mother's sister, Aunt Elaine. Before I was old enough even for school, I started working at my aunt's farm and farm market stands, same as the rest of my siblings. She grew produce, bred Great Pyrenees dogs, and raised beef cattle, but primarily she grew greenhouses full of flowers to sell.

One summer a mallard got loose and laid eggs in a potted plant next to one of Aunt Elaine's greenhouses. I found the duck eggs while I was weeding and delivered them to my aunt, who put the eggs under a nesting chicken to hatch. Sure enough, the mother hen raised the ducklings as her own. It warmed my heart to see the ducklings nuzzling under the chicken's fluffed wings—and I watched them so much that my aunt sent the ducks to live with me when they were old enough to leave their chicken mother.

I was delighted and spent hours with my nose pressed against their box on the kitchen counter, enjoying the way the ducks drank water and ate their feed like messy little babies and listening to the adorable sound of their tiny quacks. Finally I cupped each of the little ducklings in my hands and lowered them to the kitchen floor to play with my kittens, since they were about the same size. I thought they would be the best of friends, but they didn't do much playing. They all stood around looking at each other like kids at an awkward middle school dance.

I could tell right away that one of the ducklings had an underdeveloped leg, which prevented him from walking—something that was excruciatingly difficult for me. My poor Jack! Pity replaced excitement. I sat glumly on the kitchen floor next to my ducks, certain that Jack must be lonely and discouraged. I didn't understand why life would be so cruel—why he would have so much trouble walking while his siblings ran around just fine, leaving him behind without any hesitation.

And maybe that is where things got personal. I thought of the sadness and fear I'd felt when I was younger and my shoelaces had gotten tangled in barbed wire in the back field, remembered how the sound of my siblings' footsteps grew fainter and fainter and then disappeared. I already worried constantly about being left behind, being too slow or too weak, being the pale, sickly one for the rest of my life. I was so sure the duckling felt all these same things that in an inspired attempt to empower little Jack, I filled the bathtub, which had always been a place of comfort and restoration for me, with about five inches of water in the hope that he could swim better than he could walk. Maybe for the first time in his life he would be freely mobile—maybe, I thought, he could be happy. I wanted to give this experience to him. I was so eager to be the hero.

The other ducklings immediately knew what to do, diving under the water and swimming in circles around the perimeter of the bathtub, and to my delight little Jack joined right in; they were equals in the tub. But then suddenly Jack became rigid. His legs stuck out straight behind him, his wings lay limp against his side, and his eyes glazed over. I snatched up his dripping body while the other ducklings raced around the tub, quacking gleefully as if nothing was the matter.

I figured he had gotten water in his lungs, and in a moment of desperation I blew air into his little bill and pushed on his chest, like I had read vets did for other animals. I don't know if it was my attempted CPR, but the duckling came to and began behaving normally again. Relief flooded me and I loosened up too, kissing small Jack on the bill and apologizing to him a hundred times for my carelessness. Then I drained the bathwater and put the ducklings back in their newspaper-lined box in the kitchen for the night.

Later I tiptoed over to their box to peek in on them as they snuggled together, and checked the temperature of the heat lamp above them a few times before I fell asleep. But when I came downstairs in the morning, I found Jack dead. It appeared that his siblings had stepped on him continually throughout the night, because he had feed dust thick all over his rigid little body.

I guessed that Jack must still have had water in his lungs and that my little experiment had killed him after all. I knew he would have had a pretty hard life if he had survived, but that didn't bring me much comfort. I wrapped my duckling in a clean dishtowel, placed him in a shoe box, and walked out behind the corn crib to the hill that descended to the creek—the pet cemetery. It was raining, like it always rained at my funerals. Mother had told me once that rain at funerals and weddings meant God was showering blessings, so it was a good thing. I still believe that. But I also appreciated the rain that afternoon because it hid my tears. I couldn't let Mother see me cry; I knew it would break her heart, and I wanted my family to know I was up for the job. I wanted to instill confidence that I was a courageous lion who guarded the farm and its occupants, not just the sickly one like poor Jack.

So as Mother had taught me, I picked flowers for the grave and buried the box deep enough that wild animals wouldn't dig it back up. Then I stood by little Jack's grave in the rain. It felt as though whenever I tried to help an animal, they ended up no better off—or worse off—than they had been before. I struggled with wanting to give animals a better life than they could have in the wild and never being quite sure whether the more natural, even if brutal, life would be better since it was what nature intended. At least then an animal born at a disadvantage was released from a hard life early on. Still, I never could help intervening to a fault. As I walked down the hill and along the creek, I thought how unlucky this duckling was to be born with a withered leg. And I thought he was even more unlucky for having met me.

SHOTGUN

I often wondered why Mother and I were the ones most emotionally affected by the illness and death of our pets. I saw it in her eyes—recognized that same guilt I carried over each creature's suffering. I understood she felt the same guilt with us children, as though everything that went wrong was somehow her fault, even when it very clearly wasn't, like so many of my illnesses. Adding to her grief seemed cruel. Even as a child I was sensitive to her self-sacrifice and the way she pushed herself each day, raising a large family, managing the farm, and working hard at the farm market even as her aging body grew tired and arthritic. But she was tireless, always without complaint—a drive that for years I could not make sense of. All I knew was that the most tender place in my heart was for my mother, and though the passing of an animal would have a great impact on me, I understood her heartbreak would be compounded if she knew I was shaken as well.

I always tried to appear stoic and brave in front of her, then retreated deep into the woods to mourn privately. But as sneaky as I thought I was, she too knew I was sensitive, and she handled the situations delicately around me, making light of them. I suspect she was also protecting me from becoming more upset for her sake. It was a strange and awkward dance, this watchful, thoughtful restraint, but one performed out of great love and kindness.

The one time I saw Mother's compassion for animals take a darker turn was when we became the target of a group of hungry raccoons.

Joel had received an angora rabbit from a customer at the farmer's market who had adopted a few of our kittens the year before. The long-haired rabbit came home, was put into a pen, and promptly had ten babies. They all needed hutches, so before long there were rows of cages up and down the old dairy stalls.

A year later, when the rabbits were grown, Joel came down to the barn to feed and water his pets as usual. He'd filled the troughs and replaced their water when he noticed that the rabbit closest to him hadn't moved from his spot the whole time. The rabbit's gaze was fixed on him. Joel opened the pen door for a closer look and then picked the creature up, only to find him alarmingly light. The rabbit was hollow!

A raccoon had reached up through the chicken wire mesh floor and pulled the rabbit's insides out through his belly with one hand while holding the corpse by the neck with the other. What was left was a hollow rabbit shell that looked just fine from most angles, if a bit uninterested.

Then a similar thing happened to some young chickens I had been raising in the yard by the kitchen door.

During the day they roamed a small fenced area, where I could enjoy their company as I played in the yard. But at night, when predators were sure to come out, I locked them inside a large metal dog crate that Father had wrapped in two sizes of chicken wire—so tightly that I was confident no raccoon was getting its hands through any part of the enclosure. But I was wrong. A clever raccoon did indeed manage to reach in the second night, tear a chicken into small pieces right there inside the cage, and then pull the tasty pieces out to enjoy. I couldn't imagine the horror of the surviving chickens. They had probably watched the whole scene and wondered if they were next.

As cute as baby raccoons might be, we were losing too many small creatures to the hungry devils. Many people only know raccoons as cute, harmless city pests that rifle through trash bags for food, but on a farm they will hunt for meat. In fact, when raccoons are hungry enough, especially in the winter, they become more creative and ferocious than ever. They are also extremely clever, which in our eyes made them nothing less than serial killers.

Enough was enough, and one evening Mother got out the shotgun. We were astonished, and slightly amused;

it was against her nature to kill another living thing, let alone lose her cool. But the raccoon population needed to be lowered before they multiplied and the problem really got out of hand.

We started feeding the cats right in front of the kitchen door in order to lure the raccoons closer to the house. Then as night fell, we kids would peek through the windows to see if any critters had shown up to take the bait. If they had, we would run to Mother, and she would grab the shotgun. Then we would fling open the screen door while she took aim.

One particular night the raccoons just kept coming. So we propped open the kitchen door and gave Mother a chair to sit in right inside the doorway. She shot four raccoons, each about fifteen minutes apart. After a while the back porch had bullet holes in the floorboards from her shots and from Father firing at the raccoons that crept up to sniff out the kittens sleeping there.

I remember being jolted from bed a few times to the sound of the shotgun going off downstairs. After my racing heart stilled, I would think about the poor raccoons and how unfair it was that they should die, but the deaths of the poor animals they killed always pushed away the guilt before too long. Why must animals kill each other? I never wanted to accept it as nature's way, and I knew I wasn't the only one of my siblings who experienced moral conflict over the question of kill or be killed. Joel hated to kill raccoons, even after what they'd done to his pet rabbit. Once when he shot one through the lung, it hobbled off and fell over under the wisteria bush. When Joel went up to it to see if he had killed it, the raccoon gazed up at him, confused, blood coming out of its mouth before it died. The cry still haunts Joel, probably even more than the memory of picking up the hollowed-out rabbit that had been murdered by one of these creatures. At least the rabbit hadn't looked like he was begging for mercy.

RATS

R ats and mice were another story, and they were
ever present on the farm. The barn was full of
nooks and crannies, excellent places to raise a
batch of rodent babies. Food was always avail-
able from the granaries, corn crib, gardens, and fruit trees.
It was not uncommon to come across large rodents in boxes

or see them dash between shadows, and often I would find a partially eaten mouse or rat in a corner of the barn or by the side of the house. This seemed sad but natural to me, as they were nuisances that got into our storage—and they were free food for our cats.

As I grew more adventurous and explored our barn, I was amazed to discover all the different ways that rodents could look when dead. The partial mice or rats were usually hard to identify since pieces might be missing or marred. Then there were the surprisingly flat cadavers. I would pick up a crate in the barn, and there, pressed perfectly against the wood beam floor, was a preserved and seriously thin mouse. If a brave older sibling was with me, they might pick it up by the tail to discard it. I remember the sight, both funny and macabre: the stiff little body sticking straight out in the air like some strange gourmet feline popsicle. But I don't think our cats were ever interested in these, since anything edible was long gone. They were just two-dimensional mummies waiting to be uncovered.

There were also my least favorite mouse discoveries, what I called surprises. These were usually whole rodent carcasses, which we couldn't leave lying around because of the risk of disease. I also worried that if poison had taken the creature's life, it might somehow transfer to our cats. This meant we needed to scoop them up from a safe distance but still hold on firmly enough to keep the mess away from curious kittens.

One time all I had at hand were two thin sticks. I thought I could somehow use them like chopsticks to grasp the mouse, but all I did was fling the mouse a good distance and turn it over. I squealed and jumped back—the dead mouse was moving! It turned out I had uncovered the small, silent creatures intent on cleaning it out. So gross, I thought, and yet the writhing maggots were mesmerizing too. I knew they were doing an important job, but after that I always checked for slight movement and left the active carcasses for my brothers.

The invisible dead were detectable only by the occasional sour waft of air suggesting that once again, field mice escaping the harsh winter weather had found a way to die and decay unreachable inside our old farmhouse walls. When I was very young, I believed they did it on purpose— a reminder that they could not be beaten back by us or by our cats. There wasn't a lot we could do but wait it out for a week or so until the smell went away.

Usually the rats and mice were a concern only when they were dead. Then one winter the rats began to make themselves at home in our kitchen. Under the kitchen sink the 120-year-old floor had a rat hole from decades of burrowing vermin, so Father blocked it with a new board. But we could still hear them scratching at it under the sink. The cats heard it too; they would line up to listen. Mother began noticing food going missing, and when she spotted a couple of rats running across the floor at night, we decided it was time for stricter measures. I watched Joel, Steve, and Mother block off the room from the rest of the house with barricades and remove all the drawers. Then they beat at the cabinets to flush out the intruders, and as they expected, out leaped three very frantic rats. And the rats were fast—too fast. We couldn't catch them at all. So I decided to throw Coal Snow over the barricades and into the room.

Coal Snow was an old white tomcat with three or four irregular black splotches on his coat. He was also the toughest, meanest barn cat we had. Immediately he went after the rats, but it became apparent very quickly that they were going to win. They attacked him like coordinated killers, one on the underside of his neck and one on his back. We all panicked a little, and I felt almost ill over my bad call to toss the poor cat in. Joel jumped into the fray; he grabbed a spare pipe he'd unearthed from under the sink and beat the rats away from the cat. It took a lot of hits before they released poor Coal Snow. I grabbed the cat and pulled him to safety.

Once the rats were dazed enough to catch, Joel threw them into a bucket of water while we stood watching, a bit traumatized, as they drowned. It was ridiculous how large and tough those barn rats were. They were barely fazed by the pipes.

As we cleaned the kitchen afterward, we found a second hole under the gas stove, and a nest filled with chewed-up paper towels and corn silk. They had built it right next to the pilot light, where I'm sure they'd kept nice and warm. I imagined them toasting bits of food and telling scary cat stories around its glow. But now I'm amazed it didn't catch fire and burn the house down.

IAGO

Not all rats were nuisances, at least not according to my brother Paul. He had a big white rat called Iago, named after the antagonist in Shakespeare's *Othello*. Iago in the play is truly a rat. He sets up and betrays his supposed best friend, Othello, causing him to murder his own beloved wife in a jealous rage. Iago the rat didn't have murder and betrayal on his mind—not at first. And Paul was so crazy about him that he took Iago to college with him, where the white rat lived like a king.

Paul always had a flair for the dramatic, so it is likely that Iago actually started as a prop and only later became a pet. He first appeared sometime after Paul and his best friend began their role-playing game, which was odd in that only five percent of it was played in front of a computer and another five percent on game boards. The rest was played out in real life—a walking, talking improv show. They could be hanging out with friends, some players and some not, and with a subtle signal or comment, slip into character to do business, negotiate tariffs, or invade a rival's territory.

A few times they played in full costume, and as some of the players were theatre geeks, this meant elaborate costuming, props, and more. Paul's character did not believe in subtlety. His wardrobe was his Marine combat boots (for a little extra height on his six-foot-three frame) under layers of dark brown and black robes with a deeply hooded cape that moved when he swept into a room, just like the twisted old emperor in *Star Wars*. In fact, the emperor was

Paul's role model for the character. My brother carried an engraved wooden staff set with semiprecious stones, including a manufactured ruby and emerald purchased in Bethlehem on a trip to Israel in 1983, but his pièce de résistance was Iago, who at first came out only for special events like conventions, weddings, or executions.

Iago rode proudly on Paul's shoulder, his tiny claws digging into the layers of cloth to hold himself in place. And oh, the sights he saw! They'd walk across campus to the auditorium, where passersby, startled enough to see a tall robed figure bearing down on them, would get a second surprise when they turned back to gawk and noticed the huge white rat riding along on Paul's head or nestled in his hood.

When he was very young, Iago shared my gerbil's food. But rats grow up fast, and he quickly transitioned to a more refined adult menu, or as refined as college freshmen ate. This meant his diet consisted of saltine crackers and Captain Crunch lifted from the cafeteria, ramen noodles, and popcorn popped against the rules late at night in a hot oil popper. Then at some point Paul bought a bottle of root beer schnapps that was so dreadful, no one would drink it. Instead it became Iago's bottle, and he indulged in a few drops on special occasions, like when company visited and partook in nicer brews.

Iago lived in a makeshift multistory cage built from a large cardboard box filled with cereal boxes, toilet paper tubes, and other repurposed trash. Shredded newspaper covered the floor, and he maintained a nest of sorts in one hidden corner. Iago could easily have escaped by chewing or climbing his way out, but he seemed perfectly content where he was. Iago's ever-growing, ever-changing cardboard castle was the center of the dorm room, and guests would often bring him treats when they came to hang out. He appeared to love it, although that could have been the schnapps buzz.

When Paul and Iago moved back home to the farm, they shared a room with our eldest brother, Ray. But Iago wasn't ready to give up the freewheeling college lifestyle and didn't take kindly to farm rules. One night he left his cage and gnawed the plastic off all the cables for Ray's drum machine and keyboards. Ray was livid, and I think Iago could tell he was in trouble. He dug a hole in the big pot of cacti in the corner of the room, strewing dirt and gravel all over the desk and floor, and refused to come out for days.

Paul put the big pot in the middle of the floor, hoping to get him out more easily, but had no success. Then one night when Paul came into the room in the dark, he kicked the pot, and a long cactus needle went right through his tennis shoe and into his big toe. He had to cut the needle off at the shoe, then pull off the shoe and sock and dig out the needle. This particular kind of cactus breaks away at the tip like a fishhook so it can dig in deeper and seep a nasty irritant into the flesh. Paul cursed Iago's betrayal so loudly that some of us younger kids heard his yelling from all the way across the farmhouse.

Mother had already had it with hosting a fat, lazy rat in the house, and with Paul angry with Iago too, the rat was banished to the basement and then finally to the barn. Iago's new home was far from glamorous, and he received only minimal care in his old age, but he didn't seem to mind that either. I suspect socializing with barn animals wasn't too far from what he remembered from his glory days in the dorms.

I'm not sure of the exact details of his demise; it's possible he died peacefully in his sleep, dreaming of schnapps and popcorn. All we know is that one day we discovered a barn cat enjoying the remains of Iago. Paul liked to believe the cat was merely tidying up and wasn't Iago's executioner. Given my brothers' propensity to give literary names to our cats, however, that one could very well have been named Othello.

CHOCOLATE CAKE

*I*ago wasn't the only creature with an unhealthy sense of entitlement to human food. For one opossum, not even a pet, that greed did him in.

It happened the summer my brother Steve married his wife Erica barefoot on our farm, down by the spring house around the corner from the pet graveyard. She was a farm girl herself and an animal lover who worked as a vet tech, and she resembled Mother in more ways than one. Over time I watched Steve's heart grow more compassionate under her gentle influence as they collected their own hard-luck cases—creatures abandoned at the clinic where she worked.

The wedding itself was lovely. For the ceremony, Joel and Paul built a thirty-foot stone stairway that ended in a glen at the bottom of the slope. There the grass was uncut except for an aisle. We picked hundreds of daisies and stuck them in tiny vases throughout the glen and set bundles of flowers on posts at intervals all along the path. Cats and dogs roamed freely during the ceremony as guests, and Erica would have had it no other way.

Erica made a chocolate wedding cake for the occasion, in the form of a large vegetable garden with neatly arranged rows of carrots, lettuce, and vegetables made of icing. We had our fill and, as was custom, put a large portion into a Tupperware container in the giant bin freezer in the basement for them to enjoy on their first anniversary.

A month later we had a power outage, and Mother had to clean out the spoiled contents of the downstairs freezer. It took a couple of days to go through it all. The vegetable matter was wheelbarrowed to the compost pile and the meat buried. When we finally opened the Tupperware of cake late one night, we lamented the loss; we hadn't realized it was one of the victims of the outage. Mother felt terrible. We couldn't bring ourselves to throw the cake out just then, so we left it on the table outside the kitchen door.

The next morning we glanced out the kitchen window and noticed that the cake had changed overnight. In the center of the miniature garden patch was what appeared to be a very large mound of gray mold, which we assumed must have bloomed quickly in the heat. Mourning the terrible end to the cake, Mother went outside to send it off to the compost pile. But upon closer inspection she discovered that the giant mass of mold was in fact a very large opossum, lying face down in the center of the dessert. Apparently the chocolate overdose had killed him on the spot. His mouth was still full of cake.

But I couldn't feel badly for him. Erica was a spectacular baker, and death by chocolate had to be one of the better ways to go; it didn't even look like he'd stopped eating until his heart quit. He just lay there in the cake, his face covered in icing, with a smug half smile on his face.

We never told Steve and Erica.

SCHOOL DAYS

When I turned six, I was old enough to go to school with the rest of my siblings and joined the complicated operation of getting the parade of kids out of the house on time each morning. We set our alarm clocks in fifteen-minute increments and formed a queue outside the single bathroom, waiting in line for our shift. I remember mornings so cold that I would bury myself under nearby piles of laundry fresh out of the dryer—always a sure thing, as laundry was done round-the-clock in a house bursting with adventurous farm children. The moment I heard the sound of the bathroom door creaking open down the hall, I would burst from under the laundry pile and make a dash for the warm bathroom before a sibling who might have slept through their shift tried to take my place in line.

Some mornings I woke up well before my alarm and made it to the front of the queue. This was usually thanks to a cat, like cranky old gray Pascal, standing on my chest or meowing in my face, his nose pressed to mine. Sometimes instead I woke to a thud, my eyes focusing to discover Pascal tap-tap-tapping things off the dresser one by one, his gaze fixed on me as if threatening me to get out of bed...or the next porcelain cat figurine gets it!

Pascal, who was named for a famous mathematician, had grown up as a house cat in the city and had a hard time accepting his new status as an outdoor cat on a farm. Over time he grew more affectionate, or perhaps just humbled after some nights on the barn hay alongside unrefined, fleabitten country cats, but he remained a little aloof; he loved to be petted, but only in moderation. Three or four swipes down his back, and that was enough before he dismissed us with not so much as a purr for a thank you. Kind of rude, I thought. This was the first spoiled house cat ever left at the farm, and we kids weren't really sure of the protocol for interacting with such a high-class cat. Our parents continually assured us that his place was outside, same as the rest of the cats, and would put him out most nights. And then Pascal would climb in an open window in the morning, usually mine, and march back to correct us—as though there *must* be some mistake, since he was a house cat, after all.

At breakfast we youngest five sat along one side of the dining table on a wooden bench that spanned the length of the table. It was so long that the cats, when they were allowed indoors or had managed to sneak in unnoticed, squeezed in between us and piled on top of our laps, waiting for the leftover cereal milk like hungry little body warmers. Our cats gave a different kind of comfort on these mornings, a reassurance that was very welcome. We kids all felt the same sick, nervous twist in our stomachs about leaving the farm for school, which often made it hard to have an appetite.

We dealt with it in different ways. Some of us barricaded ourselves behind cereal boxes to grumpily eat our cornflakes in privacy, blocking our view of the high school– age brothers sitting opposite who couldn't resist making faces at us in response to our cranky expressions. Sometimes they resorted to disgusting antics, like Steve, who would mechanically lift spoonfuls of oatmeal into his mouth, refuse to swallow, and then unfill his mouth of oatmeal back into the bowl one gross mechanical spoonful at a time.

When we were running on time and before Mother talked Father into giving us a ride to school every morning, we would take the bus. It was a long walk down the gravel driveway to the road, and icy during the winter, but we took shelter from the wind or rain in the entrance to the brick milk house connected to the barn. When whichever older sibling was posted at the end of the driveway saw the bus appearing over the top of the hill, they would yell, "Bus coming!" and we'd all shove our kitties deeper into the barn and make a run for it. If the bus didn't see us waiting there as it descended the hill, it wouldn't stop, so we had to time it perfectly. Sometimes when we were running particularly late, one of us would notice the bus through the dining room window, and then we'd really need to bolt—we'd grab our bags, lunch boxes, and homework, yell for siblings, and run like crazy down the driveway.

None of us liked the school bus. Many of the worst kids in school lived out our way, far from the suburbs—the bullies and the mean kids. These kids would swear and smoke and pick fights with one another, and some of them even had the reputation of killing cats and dogs around Halloween. In fact, one of the reasons Mother and Father stopped being foster parents was that the neighboring boys were relentless in selling drugs to the troubled kids who came to stay with us.

Luckily for me and my siblings, our older brother Steve had come before us, and his reputation had lingered long after he'd left. Steve played electric guitar in his rock band and had long hair, muscles, and a terrifying, stone-cold gaze. He rarely said a word, but one look and any bullies knew the Voltz kids were off limits.

We were so early on the bus route that it would be

a good fifteen minutes before there was any real heat. Those were miserable mornings: sitting down by the frost-covered bus window, scraping it off poorly with a gloved hand and watching the cats leave their posts halfway down the driveway and head back into their warm barn nests. I kept my face smushed against the glass, watching it all go by: the creek's flood plain, beautiful with its layers of thin ice suspended from underbrush like tiers of a wedding cake, and winding Wolf Creek showing through the trees here and there. There was always wildlife peeking out too, a wood duck or a kingfisher, or deer if you looked closely enough. The valley was ours, and leaving it was always troubling for me.

The road sat between home and everywhere else— a powerful point of fear, transition, and change. I first understood it as a place of death thanks to all the roadkill. I remember trying to identify the dead creature before my siblings saw it in case it was a beloved pet, and I know my older siblings did the same for me.

The dead wildlife left behind horrified and fascinated me too; Rachel, always the teacher, once showed me a big black snake flattened on the road, and I remember how amazing its beautiful body looked, opened for inspection. And then how sad I was to realize that its eggs, spilled all over the road, would never hatch. That road left many small critters orphans: raccoons, deer, foxes. When trucks and cars barreled by, our iron bridge hummed and shook loudly. It was the sound of fear…and the harshness of humanity.

The school bus ride home wasn't so bad. In the afternoon the country road became the path back to our beloved farm, and when we crested the top of our valley, I could actually feel a weight lifting. I loved walking back home past the old field on the left, through swampland and forest, and over the small bridge next to our barn.

Later the road became a kind of rite of passage, a symbol of change. At first we were only allowed to ride our bikes an eighth of a mile to the nearby dirt side road and back. As our skill progressed we would attempt the two steep hills on either side of our valley. I remember Marla and I following our older brothers on one of these adventures up over the hilltop, perhaps before we were ready. As the smallest, I trailed farther and farther behind, my dread of being left alone just outside the border of our valley becoming the steam for pedaling as fast as I could.

The thrill of coasting down that hill was beautiful, though, and eventually we began exploring the surrounding roads and trails. I remember the first time I biked to a little ice cream shop a few miles away, feeling proud, independent, and a little scared when neighbor dogs barked or big trucks passed. My fondest memory of our country road was biking home in the late summer, stopping to pick wild blackberries and strawberries in neighboring fields and along the edge of the woods, and always, always listening for the sound of a small animal scurrying through the leaves into the woods, spooked by my passing. Sometimes I would drop my bike and investigate, hoping to find something cute or interesting that might let me greet it more closely.

Eventually Mother convinced Father to drive us to school in the morning since we dreaded the bus so much. Father left a stack of pre-signed late excuses on the dining room buffet next to the breakfast table, carefully written in his neat script: " ____ is late for school today because ___ was not feeling well," with a blank space for the kids' names and the date. He had all but given up hope of us ever running on time, but this was his way of adding the tiniest bit of efficiency to the mathematical equation of the mornings.

We had a twenty-minute drive to town from the farm. First we would stop at the kindergarten, then the elementary school, the junior high school, and lastly the high school. At each of the stops one or two of us would slip from the vehicle as discreetly as possible, hoping no one would notice the squealing old brown station wagon or the ugly rust-orange fifteen-passenger van—which was so big that more than once cat stowaways joined us for trips into town without any of us the wiser. We also hoped Father would turn down the loud gospel quartet 8-track when we opened the door, but of course he never did. I think Father enjoyed teasing us like this and probably loved the way we turned heads with our big, ridiculous bunch of kids and beat-up vehicles.

I was glad not to be taking the school bus anymore, though this change added a step to my morning routine: checking for kittens above the wheels and around the engine before Father started the car. Cars were a popular place for creatures to gather, especially in the bitterly cold winter, when they were drawn to the warmth of the engine and exhaust. I searched as fast as I could amid my father's firm

"Hurry, I'll be late for class." I'd seen kittens fall out injured behind us after we had started to drive, and some of the less tame cats were never found when they fled into the woods. A few we didn't even notice falling out but guessed after their disappearance that the car trip into town must have been their demise.

I often imagined what a horrible way that was to go—alone, perhaps not even missed if they were one of the shyer wild kittens that we'd never fully managed to tame. I'd remember the terror in my gut when my mother disappeared out of view at the grocery store—what if she forgot about me, with so many children to account for? One of my father's professor colleagues used to call me Number Nine when he saw me, since I was the ninth out of ten surviving children. It made me feel as though I was fading away—half-forgotten already.

That is how I thought my kittens must have felt as they watched the car continue on, leaving them in the middle of the road, far from the safety of the farm and from our family. Those were my worst fears too, so it was important to me that with the vast number of cats on the farm, they all would feel known and loved, or at least never forgotten.

We had so many casualties, accidents I could not prevent. I knew it was impossible to protect everyone and to always be at the right place at the right time. But I usually felt that I could have done something more to protect my creatures, and each death took its toll on my heart.

One of the saddest road accidents was my dog Rags, and what made it worse was that he was one of the few animals who'd tried to protect *me*. Rags was a scraggly drop-off who bounced up to us while we were playing in the field one day. I declared him my dog and named him Rags because in his natural state he looked like a pile of dirty rags. I spent a lot of time pulling burrs out of that mess of fur.

Mother wasn't too happy with Rags at first because he liked to steal tomatoes while we prepared them for canning. But then soon after he came to live with us, he followed us down to the creek, where he saw us all yelling and screaming in play. Alarmed, he dove in and swam over to me, pulling me by my shirt to the safety of the shore. That was when Mother decided we could keep him. That summer we ran together in the tall grass of the field, having all kinds of adventures. I remember the way Rags, being a short dog, would bounce like a rabbit so he could see where he was going over top of the grass and daisies.

Early one Easter morning my parents brought me into their room and sat me on the bed to tell me Rags had been hit by a car. Apparently the neighbor boy who had killed the dog felt just awful delivering the news on a holiday morning. I think Mother and Father did too; they gave me a little stuffed Easter bunny to remember him by, and I named it Rags.

It was highly unusual to get such a gift, especially when it wasn't Christmas or my birthday; we didn't have a lot of money for extras, and my parents knew that if just one of us got a special treat, it wasn't fair to the rest of the children. But I understood what they were trying to do. I held that stuffed rabbit tight, imagining the hug somehow extended to the real Rags, wherever he might be now.

Nature was a harsh threat to our animals, to be sure, but the dangers we created with our roads and machinery seemed just as bad. Occasionally I had the pleasure of knowing I had prevented an accident, and that brought me peace and renewed my appreciation for whichever cat had been spared. Just like the creatures that had recovered from illnesses, the rescued kitty would get extra attention and snuggles for at least a few days. I remember trying to explain to various animals why their actions had put them in danger and how they should do things differently the next time. I'm not sure they listened all that well, but at the very least, I hoped to make up for our part.

KERM'S CATS

I took my philanthropy to neighboring farms too, with mixed results. Our neighbors a mile down the road, Kermit and Sally, were dairy farmers who lived in a pale-green farmhouse decorated in a cow theme. On Mondays we youngest children would clean out a dozen milk jugs, pile in the station wagon— piloted by Father or one of our older brothers—and head over to the dairy. Kerm gave us all the milk we wanted in exchange for permission to harvest the hay from our fields. I never liked the taste of the heavy cream or the smell of the milk tank, but Marla continually reminded me to suck it up because the milk was free.

And I did not really mind going, because I loved seeing the neighboring farm's cats. It was like a whole other cat city just down the road from us. The cats there were less friendly, more skittish than ours, I thought, but seeing the difference between the two gave me the satisfaction of knowing that all the time and affection I invested into our cats made a difference in their quality of life.

Kerm did not seem to like cats any more than Father did, though he appreciated their help attending to the mouse population; and they, in return, enjoyed the free milk. Still, he had little patience for cats that got in the way of real work. Kerm had a rule that if cats didn't move, they got run over. When I saw his tractor rolling up, I would rush around gathering sunbathing kittens under my arms, trying to look casual since I wanted to be respectful of his farm's rules and not get in his way either. A part of me wondered if his no-tolerance rule applied to small children as well, but it wasn't worth the risk of finding out.

I stopped riding along on milk day after an incident involving me knocking over the fence and letting the cows out, but it wasn't quite as simple as that. I was sitting in the back seat of our parked Toyota while we waited for Ray and Joel to finish filling the milk jugs. Marla was in the front passenger seat, ignoring me despite my efforts to get her to listen to whatever school story I was rambling on about. After leaning farther and farther forward, trying to get into Marla's line of vision, I bumped the stick located between the two front seats, knocking the car out of gear. Parked on a hill, it slid backward down the slope, over a flower bed, and straight through the pasture fence. Ray and Joel ran out of the milk house, scrambling to contain the escaped cows, but Kerm didn't seem concerned, as my brothers were quick to repair the fence and return the cattle to their pasture. But I knew Father wouldn't be happy about the whole disgrace-ful ordeal, so I stayed in my room for the rest of the evening.

Although I avoided Kerm's farm after that day, I still rode my bike past it often enough. I think I kept hoping for a glimpse at their kitties again, but my attention was usually devoted to outspeeding Kerm's dogs—Bullet and Laudie, both labs, and Joe the Doberman—who chased me the entire length of their pastures, barking every time the crunching sound of my tires over country road came into range of their acute hearing. The pack had been friendly enough when we visited on milk day, greeting us at our car with wagging tails. But perhaps seeing me on my bike, they did not recognize me—or worse, I worried, they did. In any event, I did not appreciate the three of them announcing my presence after what I'd done to the fence.

I wished Kerm's cats the best, and sure enough, most of them seemed to survive just fine. When Kerm eventually died of cancer and the dairy farm was sold, some of his cats traveled through the woods to our farm. I recall three skittish tomcats in particular that preceded the litters of matching kittens we found in the barn later that season.

MONET AND PANCAKE

W e didn't have air conditioning, so during the summer I slept with my window open. Pascal, and other cats over the course of the years, would climb up a tree adjacent to the house and then onto the kitchen roof, which crested outside my second-floor window. Usually they would stay to socialize before sneaking downstairs to the kitchen, but sometimes I would go out to join them on the roof to watch the sun rise. As the farmhouse was on top of a small hill at the base of a valley, the view was spectacular from my rooftop vantage point. To my right were blossoming apple and cherry trees full of bird feeders, and beyond that the wood pile, where cats perched high to watch the birds. Next came rows of daffodils and prickly raspberry bushes, and then the large vegetable garden that we hoed and weeded relentlessly on hot summer days. It was tiring work, but nothing beat the satisfaction of picking from the lush garden before dinner—sometimes spoiling my appetite on green beans and cherry tomatoes as I went.

Past the vegetable garden stood a row of walnut and oak trees, and then open fields of tall grass and daisies. I often stomped paths through these fields using an awkward sidestep-and-press action that worked surprisingly well, often stopping to flatten a small circle, like a private grass and wildflower fortress. I loved the idea of being completely hidden from the world, lost to time. But in retrospect I'm sure the pack of cats and occasional dog that followed me were a dead giveaway to my whereabouts.

Mother was gardening near the house early one summer day when a short-haired black tortoiseshell calico cat appeared out of the woods, weaving back and forth across the path I'd trod in the grass. Something seemed to be wrong. The cat didn't look hurt, but she zigzagged across the lawn and bumped into wheelbarrows and children's toys as she gingerly felt her way toward the house, like she was following the sound of my mother.

Sure enough, once she felt Mother's leg against her side, the cat began rubbing against it and broke into contented purring. Upon closer examination Mother recognized the thick glaze over her eyes. The cat was blind, but her intuition had brought her to the very person who would keep her safest.

Because this was during the period when we named all our cats after artists and composers, we called the sweet cat Monet—not only for her vision impairment, but also because of the pattern on her coat, which resembled paintbrush strokes. It's hard to say how long the blind cat had been traveling. The part of the woods she had come from was not near the road, and she would have had to pass through swamp marshes to cross it. It would have been difficult for her not to get stuck in the deep mud, but now that she had managed to make her way here, we could hardly ask her to leave again. So Monet became a new favorite pet.

Monet was happy and overly trusting for being blind. She dashed around the farm full of confidence despite how often she ran into farm equipment, toys, and other objects whose locations changed frequently. But she was a chore to take care of since she didn't groom herself like the other cats and would get infections or botflies nesting in her flesh.

I remember the first time I saw this dreadful pestilence. The sun shone through the fresh laundry on the line, and I was met by Monet, who was purring peacefully despite a deep, gaping hole in her side. Terrified, I ran to my mother, sure that the cat was going to die right away. Mother cleaned out the wound, and I was shocked to see what I thought were wriggling grubs inside.

I had seen grubs unearthed during gardening and had learned to still the feelings of disgust and take time to observe and enjoy the unique behavior of these not-yet-matured creatures. I would carry them on leaves into the weeds to find them a new home or cover them back up with

soil. I never thought of these small things as infants, creatures to protect, but rather belonging to a special stage and
at least worth understanding.

But botflies were different in my mind, a direct attack on something I loved. The audacity of such a disgusting creature invading my precious pets horrified me enough
that I had secret conversations in my head about why terrible things were allowed to happen and whether it was okay
to hate them. I never did quite figure it out.

Even though Monet recovered quickly, my mind
was opened to yet another enemy intent on harming my
wards, and that summer I petted my cats constantly for any
strange new bumps that might be maggots under the skin.
I had read how the flies would sometimes lay their eggs on
healthy skin so the larvae could burrow down and feast
on their host's flesh. I knew these parasites would not kill
an animal, but the resulting wounds and weakness could
cause big problems, so I dealt with them promptly. Mother
and I covered the air holes with a thick layer of petroleum
jelly to force the larva to the surface for oxygen, and that
usually did the job. I do not remember if Mother had to
make any incisions, but I trusted her experience as she fear-

lessly tended the wounded. I felt proud and a little nervous whenever I got to help her.

It confused me that the cats did not seem to notice the problem. They followed their usual patterns, seemingly unaware that part of their leg or stomach was missing—so unreal, like furry, purring zombies. One of my siblings told me they thought the maggots secreted some kind of numbing agent, but now I wonder if our cats were just tough. Monet certainly was.

While she managed to stumble around and take care of herself well enough, Monet could never quite manage motherhood. She would simply forget where she had birthed the kittens or neglect to lick their air passages clear after birth. Usually by the time I realized she'd given birth to her litter, they had already died. The newborn kittens were always scattered around the farm as if she had decided to take a walk in between birthing each one. I remember collecting their cold little bodies early in the morning, praying that the chilly rain had come after they had passed away. I tried to make out their fur colors to see if they had been as beautiful as their mother. These fragile kittens had needed a good midwife, and their loss made me feel like I had failed them and Monet.

I thought that Monet deserved companionship in her dark world, especially after all her loss, and I was determined to help her have the kittens that she wanted. Selfishly I was excited by the idea of small black tortoiseshell calicos. It was a new coat color palette for the farm, where most of the cats were brown, orange, or peach, and sometimes black or the predominately white variety of calico.

After the first lost litter, I tried caging Monet when she was late in her next pregnancy. She never seemed to remember the bars were there, though, and would walk into them continuously, injuring herself. This made me anxious, so instead I let her free and watched her carefully. Unfortunately I probably wasn't careful enough. I don't remember how many more times she attempted motherhood, but I do remember that the last time she was pregnant she gave birth to only one kitten, who almost miraculously survived his birth and infancy under the careful watch of my mother and me.

I was delighted for Monet, who had gotten her wish and was finally a mother—and she appeared happier than ever, licking him for hours on end, purring her head off. At first they stayed in a box in the house until the kitten grew stronger and the weather warmer. Monet seemed to appreciate the time and extra attention, and even after they moved outside, she kept her kitten in a nook right by the kitchen door so they would still be close to us.

The kitten was a mess of long, woolly gray fur because Monet would lick him in random spots instead of methodically moving all around. It seemed like every time we saw the funny little guy, he would have one or two new cowlicks surrounded by unkempt fur. Sometimes it got bad enough that we would help out with the grooming when we could.

This was Pancake. Pancake got his name because of the way his doting blind mother learned to keep track of him: she would sit on him. He survived to adulthood a perfectly happy cat, though he always walked like a cowboy who'd been riding a horse all day, running with his back legs sprawled far apart. I remember dressing Pancake up in my fashionable sister Renee's white lacy slips, which resembled silk gowns once I'd fashioned a ribbon belt around his waist, and putting pearls around his neck. I'd thought he would be elegant because of his long, beautiful fur. Instead he looked rather unladylike as he waddled away, despite his fine attire.

Monet lived longer than most of our cats, which I have always found surprising since she had the disadvantage of being blind. She died peacefully in her favorite box of hay in the downstairs barn one winter. After I'd noticed her slowing down, I would nervously check on her throughout the day, scared each time that I would find her curled up, lifeless. Sometimes I chose not to check on her because I was worried about what I might find, and then I would feel guilty for neglecting her, allowing her to lie there all alone in the dark. When I visited, I would briefly talk to her and touch her so she knew someone was there—and she would respond affectionately every time, in spite of her exhaustion. But I often wondered if it was cruel to wake her up to pet her and then leave her shortly afterward. Did she feel lonely, confused? Did she long to be petted more? When she eventually passed on, it was bittersweet.

Pancake, too, had a longer-than-average lifespan for a barn cat. He might have lived longer had we not accidentally backed over him with the station wagon when my parents were taking some of us kids to town. We didn't even notice at the time. Joel, who had stayed home, found

Pancake on the driveway and knew he had to clean it up. He laid the fluffy gray cat in a box and buried him on the hill before we got back. Later Steve made an insensitive joke that Pancake was now flat as a pancake, and I remember feeling bothered by it but also glad we could pretend to laugh about the whole thing. It was all so terrible, and yet I didn't want to see my mother sad. Even more, I didn't want her to see that I was sad.

It's strange, the way I vividly remember these animals' pain as if I had experienced it myself. The first week after each death, I would flee into my room or the woods to cry, and even years afterward I would still cry at the thought of each friend as they entered my mind. As a small child I wondered if death would get easier. Eventually it did, a bit, my sensitivity fading little by little. A survival tactic, perhaps, or just the effect of time and age. Though with that came another loss: my intuition and my awe of the magic around me. But I was more able to tuck all the painful thoughts into a safe place in the back of my head, a place I could return to in order to deal with them at a more convenient time or simply leave them until they faded into my subconscious.

NORMAN

As with everything on the farm, life quickly replaced loss. I will never forget the winter night Norman was sent to us. It was late, and Renee was reading to me on the patched leather sofa in the living room while I waited for my turn in the bath, when we heard a tiny kitten calling inquisitively at the front door. It's funny how cats and even some dogs master the sound of a question, their voices rising a note higher at the end of their meow or woof when they're asking to be let inside or be pet. Renee and I looked at each other curiously; it was rare to find kittens on the farm in the dead of winter. But I was full of hope. Just a day or two earlier, tragedy had struck the farm when a highly contagious disease wiped out all of the cats, even the hardiest toms. I was still heartbroken and longed for a little creature on which to shower my love. I jumped off the couch, barely daring to believe our good fortune.

The second we opened the door to peek, a gust of freezing cold wind and snow rushed in, and almost as quickly a tiny snow-white kitten with ridiculously large ears. The kitten ran straight for the kitchen with surprising confidence—how odd that she knew exactly where to go for food. It was clear right away that this was going to be a house cat.

Norman was obviously a drop-off, because none of our barn cats had ever given birth to a white kitten. But Mother informed Father that Norman was an angel sent from heaven and therefore should be allowed to stay in the house. I suspected Mother knew how terribly we kids wanted a house cat, and this was her way of telling Father it was time to let us have our wish, whether or not she actually believed Norman was an angel. But I did find the kitten's timing suspicious, appearing so soon after what I considered a horrid massacre. Was this tiny apparition sent from God, or was the ghost-white cat the angel of death? Well, white except for the big grease stain she sported on top of her head between her disproportionately large ears.

It didn't take long for us to realize that something was not quite right with Norman; she seemed to have difficulty with equilibrium or depth perception. This wasn't surprising, since many of the drop-offs that reported to our front door were left there because they had health problems. Blind, deaf, diseased, pregnant—all won a ticket to the farm. But I don't think they felt abandoned, because each one was greeted with squeals of excitement. In our eyes their flaws made them unique and all the more precious.

That was particularly true of Norman. Throughout her life Norman had a grease stain on top of her head, just like she had the day she arrived, from walking under cars and bumping her head against the undercarriage. She wasn't blind, like Monet; I'm still not sure what was wrong with her, though it's possible she was thrown from the car when she was dropped off and damage was done to her head. All I know is that she was used to it and didn't appear to mind. Norman was a very happy cat.

We treated her like royalty despite her awkward gallop, not at all like a normal cat's run. Norman would trot through our living room and attempt to scoot under the coffee table, but instead she would bonk her head underneath it, fall over, and then use that momentum to swing up into a lounging position and begin grooming herself, completely unfazed. She could never just lie down gracefully either, but would tip to one side like a tree falling over, sometimes landing with one leg high in the air. The whole process almost looked choreographed. It was very entertaining.

It took at least a month for Norman's name to settle. Each of us had a different idea: Joel, with his passion for botany, wanted to call her Trillium after the rare white wildflower we searched for in the woods every spring. Mother wanted to call her Angel, possibly to persuade Father to continue keeping the cat in the house. But no one could agree, and she remained nameless until Steve made a bet that he could get the name Norman to stick merely by using it consistently. It did stick. She was Norman as long as she lived.

Norman had been separated from her mother too early, before she was done nursing, so she had developed an oral fixation. Just like Linus in *Charlie Brown*, she had a fuzzy blue blanket and would nurse it passionately, massaging it with her paws, purring, and leaving giant wet saliva patches. When she wasn't sleeping on her blue blanket, Norman would snuggle up in my bed, her body under the covers like a human and her head on the pillow next to me. She would turn toward me so we were face to face, then purr loudly, almost smiling with her eyes. Sometimes I liked this, but sometimes it made me feel a little uncomfortable; the closeness I found unnerving. I imagined this was what being married was like.

Before long Norman caught one of the diseases that could wipe out a whole cat population—most likely feline distemper. Just like the other cats, she lost her appetite entirely, ran a fever, and lay almost lifeless on her blue blanket, which I twisted into a nest for her. I placed her on the couch so I could sleep next to her and mixed canned cat food with vitamin paste and water, force-feeding her using an eyedropper. The vitamin paste had enough calories to improve a cat's energy, which was usually the biggest hurdle; a cat that did not eat did not have the strength to fight illness. Sometimes Norman swallowed the drops, but sometimes she did not, and then I had to wipe her messy face, neck, and blanket clean as the fluid dripped out. It was a heartbreaking process. I apologized to Norman, crying as I pleaded with her to swallow. The entire time I prayed to God to heal our angel cat, promising all kinds of things in return, like being a better helper around the house.

Mother and I nursed her day and night, even though we were sure she wasn't going to survive. Yet on the third day she started to improve and after that seemed to be immune to the disease. Norman's resilience was astounding for the remainder of her life; she stayed healthy through two more epidemics that took out many of the other cats.

Much as with people, Norman's quirks became exaggerated with age. She grew progressively weirder, and with every year that went by, her tongue stuck out farther and farther. She was an odd sight with her giant ears, lanky body, tongue sticking out a good half inch, and complete lack of grace. A school friend once painted a depiction of what Norman would have looked like if she were human: a weathered old woman wearing too much makeup, a cigarette hanging out of her mouth and a glass of hard liquor in her hand. True, Norman was rough around the edges, but we considered her the queen of the farm, and she had the most beautiful kittens.

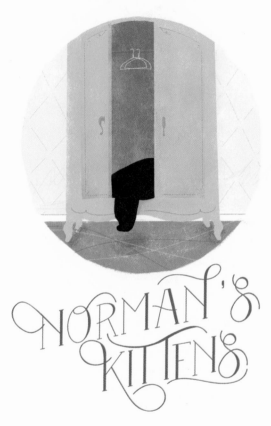

NORMAN'S KITTENS

orman loved having kittens, and she insisted that my mother and I be at her side for the entire labor and birth. I had never seen a cat demand an audience for birthing kittens before, and haven't since. When she knew it was time, she would come find me, do the mother cat call, and lead me to the spot she had picked, looking over her shoulder every so often to make sure I was right behind her. If I didn't follow right away, she would keep running back and forth between me and her blanket until I dropped what I was doing and went with her before the kittens were born right there in the hall.

When the kittens started to come, I would call for Mother downstairs. She would hurry in with a warm, wet cloth, congratulating Norman like a proud midwife. Mother would pull the birth sack off each kitten, wipe their noses and faces so they could breathe, and then put them next to Norman's face for a cleaning all over. Norman was pleased with herself, I could tell—her eyes were so happy and squinty as she purred, almost like she was smiling.

The kittens were always gorgeous. Some were short-haired or long-haired white with one green and one blue eye, some gray and white, some black, some calico, and a few times orange, depending on which tomcat had visited that season. She had over eighty of them in her lifetime, but I think we may have only ever kept one kitten, because they were so easy to find homes for.

After many years Norman became too old to carry

kittens to full term, and the last couple of pregnancies resulted in stillbirths. She must not have felt the labor coming, because she didn't call for me until they were already born. I followed her anxiously—I knew it was early in the pregnancy—and sure enough, I found them in my bed in a puddle of blood. It particularly saddened me that even though the two kittens were too frail to have possibly survived the birth, Norman purred and showed them off to me, a proud mother full of love.

Norman had a kitten void that was strongest after miscarriages. But several times she was blessed with adopted kittens shortly after losing her own.

I will always remember her joy the first time this happened. A stray cat had given birth to a litter of orange kittens at a church acquaintance's house, and Mother reluctantly offered to adopt them. When we got home, I placed the mewing box in the middle of the living room floor and called out the front door for Norman, curious what she would do; she had recently suffered another miscarriage and had plenty of milk to nurse. The moment Norman came inside the house, her ears pricked up at the kitten cries, and she rushed around, her eyes wide. When she tracked down the location of the mewing, she actually jumped into the tall box and started to care for them as though they were her own kittens that she had merely misplaced. Some of the kittens were startled and hissed at her, but they quickly warmed up to their adopted mother and her milk.

JONAH

Norman's last adopted kitten was another miracle, Jonah. While I was out in the backyard one summer afternoon, I heard the fearful cries of a small kitten far off in the woods toward the road. My instincts kicked in, and though I could tell this was not a kitten of mine, I knew by the kitten's tone that she did not feel safe. So I hurried through the yard, past the pet cemetery, and along the creek, calling out in my imitation of a mother cat's call to comfort her until I could find her. I scanned the underbrush along the swamp and followed the sound of the kitten as she began calling back to me, loud over the trickling creek.

When I first noticed the tiny kitten, she was already frantically swimming across the creek toward me. I ran to the edge to intercept her, but the kitten pulled herself out of the water and onto the muddy shore. Her shiny black-and-white coat was slick over her small frame, but she began purring the moment I picked her up.

Who could throw such a tiny kitten into a swamp? Had she been tossed in the creek to drown? As I pondered this, she shivered with cold and, as far as I could tell, excitement that someone had come to her rescue. I held her close to keep her warm and did my best to pat her dry on my shirt, then carried her up the weedy slope of the creek to the house. There she was enthusiastically greeted by Norman, who was only too delighted to take on the duties of motherhood.

We named the little runt Jonah because she was

delivered from the water, though her name soon morphed into Jo-Jo. Since Mother considered Jonah another miracle cat, and Norman had claimed the small kitten as her own, Jonah was welcomed into the fold of those few household cats and settled in just fine.

My younger brother Jesse became quite attached to her, something I'd never seen him do with a pet before. This was during his couch gymnastics phase, and he taught Jo-Jo backflips and how to jump to chase a string. First he would lead Jo-Jo quickly across the floor in an arc, then at the last moment flick the string up into the air. The cat would jump three feet straight up and flip in the air, heading back the way she came. I'm still not sure how she managed to change direction midair. Jesse's arm was always covered in her accidental scratches, but they were quite the gymnastic duo. The two would jump from couch to coffee table to chair together, playing "the floor is lava," and Jo-Jo seemed to get the concept of the game pretty well. Or perhaps she just liked imitating Jesse's movements.

THE
GREAT
INDOORS

B y this time I was starting high school and spent a good amount of time with school band, choir, and drama productions, just as all my older siblings had. Music had always been a part of our family, a trait handed down through the generations. Most of us played an instrument, some of us extremely well, and song seemed to burst from any room at any time. I myself preferred accompanying the others on my flute or singing privately, since I was so accustomed to disappearing into the background. I would sing in the woods, in the high rafters of the barn, or in the old silo, with its eerie acoustics.

My only audience would be whichever cats had followed me, but I preferred my small sidekicks. During one of my private performances, Marla cracked the door behind me and listened to the sad good-bye song I was making up on the spot for the kitten sitting in front of me on the old wooden porch steps. I recall tearing up as I sang to my small friend about how much I would miss him when he went to his new home, probably a cousin's house, later that day. To my horror Marla threw open the door behind me midphrase, knowing she had caught me in a vulnerable and embarrassing moment. I took my kitten under my arm and slunk away to finish my song in peace.

Not surprisingly, our love of music grew into a love of theatre, and over the years my siblings became mainstays in various school productions. While my parents did not like the idea of us spending more time off the farm than we needed to, my older siblings fought this battle for us and largely won our parents over. I think after Mother and Father saw the gift their eldest children had for theatre, they knew it was hopeless to keep us off the stage. In any event, by the time I entered high school it was a given that I would be involved in theatre, and I found myself enjoying the outside world a bit more, or at least a fantasy version of it. Theatre was an easier place to relate to other kids my age who otherwise I didn't have much in common with. And it was a chance to be in the spotlight for the first time in my life. We were a house full of hermits with the paradoxical desire to lift our voices and be heard.

Jesse—the baby of the family—felt the same way. He and I were not talkative people, and both of us had all but given up getting a word in at home, especially around our exuberant eldest three siblings. Eventually we took comfort in not being expected to speak; I appreciated that I could easily sneak away to a quieter, four-legged crowd, and Jesse would head to his room to play games. It became a running joke that at some point halfway through dinner, one of us would realize Jesse wasn't at the table anymore but in his room continuing his video game. The kid was stealthy.

As much as I loved the escape of theatre, I still preferred to be on the farm, at least between performances. But in a strange twist, spending time outside the farm opened my eyes to some of what I'd never noticed close to home. I'd long seen the run-down farmhouses in the countryside, some in such bad shape that I prayed no one actually lived there. It wasn't until I was making the rounds to sell fruit as a fundraiser for our marching band, that I discovered many of these farms were in fact inhabited. The poverty was devastating, even to me, coming from a poor farm myself. I remember the sick feeling that I had been blind to all this need in the farmland surrounding us. My compassion had always been limited to my animals. On the school bus ride home, one girl was always especially mean, even to me on occasion, though I sat quietly and kept to myself. But one afternoon, after she had been particularly rude, I got home and wept, imagining what kind of life she had that made her so miserable, so cruel to others. My heart broke for her.

By now, just as I had started to evolve, so had the farm. Less effort was put into production; animals like cows were not as important anymore, though we still dealt with them on our aunt's farm, where we spent our summers working. Most of our animals were around for enjoyment or rescue rather than necessity, and even the eggs the chickens laid were more an add-on to those bought from the store or the market.

The family dynamics had changed too. Half of my siblings had moved away at this point, lessening the amount of food and clothes required. Rachel, Marla, and I started receiving small pets, like birds, fish, small rodents, chameleons, and hermit crabs as presents on birthdays. In fact, the house was becoming overrun with small critters, and I spent a lot of time rushing to catch escaped gerbils in a dead heat with a hungry house cat or separating baby guppies from the tank before the adult fish devoured them. Even inside the farmhouse, the circle of life was in full motion. I feel Norman and Pascal helped us with this transition, being the pioneers of the house pet concept.

HARRY

Our farm entered a new era with Harry, the first cat I ever took to the vet.

Like so many of my favorite cats, Harry was orange and tiger striped, and incredibly soft. But the unusual thing about him was how expressive his face was. Harry would lock eyes with us and squint in a way that made us feel he was telling us how much he loved us. I swear he was even smiling. Previous house cats had enjoyed our company and appreciated that we offered them a warm house and food, but Harry was the first who behaved as though he liked us for who we were, no strings attached.

Harry seemed to need love just as much as any creature needed food or water, and he was more than happy to give love back. He would wrap his arms around my neck and kiss me on the lips every chance he got, which was strange at first; we had never had a hugging cat before, and I was never a hugging type of person, at least not with people. But I remember how when Harry hugged me, I would think how good it felt. He was patient with other cats too and would often help raise the litters of kittens that came through the house, though some of them would be confused and a little disappointed when they'd root for nipples on his fuzzy orange belly and find nothing. I never saw him fight with another cat either, like most tomcats would. He was an exceptional male cat.

This was all the more surprising, given his rough start. Harry was born to one of the wild calico barn cats, and he was the most ill-natured kitten of the litter. He was also terrified of people. When Joel tried to catch him before he went wild, Harry would have none of it; he growled and flashed his claws, pure hate apparent on his face, then sank his teeth and claws deep into Joel's hand. Joel screamed and let go of the kitten, who bolted for the open cellar door at the end of the garage. My brother shook off the pain and lunged toward the kitten again, who looked at his options and decided to jump straight off the seven-foot staircase into the dark cellar. Joel ran downstairs and found the kitten wedged between a beam and the cellar wall, still thrashing his claws furiously. The moment Joel unstuck him, the kitten scampered under the enclosed stairwell, where he could not be reached.

The kitten cowered under those stairs for a week. I left food and water but was unable to draw him out of his hiding place, not even with my mother cat call. When he finally decided to emerge from the basement of his own free will, he was quite different from the wild, clawing cat-demon we'd seen earlier. Harry, as Joel promptly named him, rubbed his body against our legs and then scooted over to me as though he were desperate for my love, purring as soon as I picked him up. From that day forward, Harry was the sweetest, most affectionate cat we'd ever had.

Because Harry was so special to us, I grew particularly worried when his health began declining unexpectedly. The usual procedure was to go to the local farming supply store and buy antibiotics, ointment for wounds, and eyedroppers for feeding and hydrating. None of these did any good. He became lethargic, feverish, and thin—and unhappy, something we had not seen since he was a kitten. I realized that for this cat's spirit to be broken, he must truly be in bad shape, and for the first time in my life I asked Father to drive me and Harry to the vet.

I had a little money saved up from working at my aunt's farm. Usually when I had money to spare, I picked up a seventeen-pound bag of cat food for the pantry, since I suspected Mother only kept half the farm cats around because I loved them so much. We'd never considered the luxury of a vet visit before, but this was more than just a sick cat; Harry had become a joy to all of us. My mother and my siblings were happier for having him around. It wasn't merely about my heart breaking, but about theirs too, and I couldn't bear that. I thought this would be his salvation and that the money for the appointment would be well spent.

In the clinic's waiting room, Harry lay still in a ripped old bath towel on my lap. Father sat next to me, pulling out a highlighter and one of the paperback alternative science books he always had ready in his pocket. Town people waited too, with their expensive-looking pet carriers and even more expensive-looking pets. The smell of chemicals from sanitizing products stung my nose. I felt vulnerable, out of place—like Dorothy waiting to see the wizard. I had put so much blind faith in this man.

We were called into the exam room, and the vet looked Harry over grimly. Then he informed me that my cat had leukemia and strongly suggested that I put him to sleep. My heart crumbled. I had spent the past hour wondering how soon my dear Harry might feel himself again. There was no way I was bringing Harry's lifeless body home to my family after they, like me, had invested so much hope into his journey to town. They hadn't even had the chance to say good-bye.

Putting animals out of their misery was not a new concept for me. When we found a cat torn apart by stray dogs or seriously injured by cars and knew there was no hope, Father or Mother would carry them down into the barn. I would pray frantically for the animal's comfort and peace, covering my ears until the gunshot rang out. And then I would sit still, waiting in the eerie silence until I heard the sound of gravel crunching as my mother or father walked up the driveway with a closed box. If I looked upset, they would assure me the pet was relieved of their pain instantly. I hoped with all my heart that this was true.

But Harry was a friend who had given back to us unconditionally, and I wouldn't put him down without doing everything I could to nurse him or at least make him comfortable. I told the vet I'd think about euthanasia, but for now I was taking Harry home. The fee was sixty dollars, which Father paid in my place when he saw how upset I was. It's possible that was his plan all along, though I knew he wouldn't want the other kids to find out. Otherwise we'd all be lining up in front of him with every variety of ill creature, domestic or not, asking for a ride to the vet. I felt terrible about taking Father's money after I had promised him that I would pay, but I was also grateful. Sixty dollars sounded like a fortune to me.

I held my cat close as Father drove us home. I cried for Harry, trying desperately to hide it, but I had given up hope. Harry cried in pain, and to punctuate the moment, he had diarrhea on my lap. I don't think that my father said a word the whole trip to or from the vet—or while we were there, for that matter. Stoic, as always. I was glad he didn't say anything about the crying or the foolish errand.

Despite his leukemia diagnosis, Harry appeared to improve over the course of a week or so and returned to his happy and loving self, though he was still quite thin. I kept a close watch on him and bought a tube of high-calorie vitamin paste, which he enjoyed the taste of thoroughly. Though he certainly wasn't back at a hundred percent, his spirits seemed high, and I allowed myself to relax a little.

Harry made it through another season in decent health. Christmas came, and he stole baby Jesus out of the manger scene under the Christmas tree and hid the figure, just like he had every year before. But when winter arrived in full force, Harry vanished. Mother assured me it was likely he had gone on a quest, as most tomcats do, and would return. But Harry wasn't as strong as he used to be, and the snow was deep. I searched the farm and the fields for paw tracks in the snow, but with little luck, and soon another heavy snowstorm passed through and there were no traces left to look for. Still I searched to the back of the fields and along the edge of the woods with a flashlight, calling his name. No reply. I did this every cold evening and during snowstorms, when I worried for him most, but as the winter wore on I had to give up. He was clearly no longer nearby.

It wasn't until nearly spring that the snow melted and Mother informed me she had found Harry's body at the side of the road, just feet from our driveway. He had likely been there since the first day he went missing, preserved under layers of snow and ice. I told Mother that a quick death from a car was a better way to go than the slow effects of leukemia, which was sure to have gotten worse over time. I wasn't sure if what I told her was completely true, but I hoped it was and tried to take comfort in the thought.

I had always assumed it was physiological damage that changed Harry's personality when he jumped off that staircase landing as a kitten. Looking back, I suppose he had just reached a point of brokenness and needed our love. I'm glad we gave it to him. To Harry, that was as important as anything in life.

HANGING DOG

T he more time I spent at school, the more I missed on the farm. Sometimes new animals came and went so fast that I never even noticed them. As much as that bothered me, I knew my life was changing; it finally sank in that I could not be there every time I thought I should be. Occasionally I would mention to Mother that I hadn't seen a certain pet about, and she would, in the most gentle way possible, explain how it had passed away or disappeared days or even weeks before. I was seeing less tragedy firsthand now, which allowed reason to get the upper hand over emotions. I began to accept that many things would always be out of my control. And over time I grew a deeper understanding of how animals were partly a product of their environment and how sometimes we simply couldn't save them, whether physically or otherwise, no matter how hard we tried.

Joel, who was in the habit of sleeping with his head next to the open window in the summer, woke up one morning to what he thought was the sound of a child lost in the woods. He got out of bed, pulled on his old boots, and hiked into the forest, following the noise. What he ended up seeing was a baby deer standing by the side of the road as she cried over her dead mother and brother.

Before long Mother and I woke as well, and the three of us tried for a while to catch the fawn, which was only as big as a cat. At one point Mother managed to hold a bottle of baby animal formula in front of her long enough for the fawn to have a taste, but the creature took off again before we could grab her. Since we had no experience re-habilitating deer, Mother called the game commission, who said they would shoot the deer if they came out. She told them to never mind.

She then called a couple of Native American men she had heard of who specialized in rehabilitating wild-life, and they arrived promptly. The two men prayed over the dead mother deer and made a fire to release her spirit, then easily caught and swaddled the baby deer and took her away in their car. I was sad to see the fawn go, since in the short time I'd spent tracking her through the woods, I'd imagined her growing tame and playing in the yard by my side. But once the car drove away I felt relieved, like I knew for sure the fawn would be okay. She was in better hands and would someday return to the woods to live the life she was meant for.

The most difficult lesson was learning to cope with the powerlessness, especially when our human efforts were simply too small to fight the magnitude of an animal's hurt. Our neighbor down the road, who also happened to be my dentist, had the drop-off problem too, even though he did not own a farm but a large estate. While working in his garden one day, he saw a van stop on the road in front of his house and leave behind a cat, a dog, and a potbellied pig. There was even a moment of eye contact between him and the van driver before it took off. People were getting bolder! The pig, oddly enough, made himself at home in my neighbor's house, and the cat was comfortable outside, but our neighbor called Mother, asking her if we could provide a home for the dog. Mother did not want to adopt another dog but agreed to take him to be helpful. After all, it wasn't like our neighbor was given a choice in the matter either.

I did not know about any of this until my dentist appointment shortly afterward. The dentist asked my mother how the dog was, and my mother answered, "Just fine!" I had not yet heard of this dog, so after the dentist left the waiting room, I begged for details. She shushed me and promised that she would tell me about it later, which I knew couldn't be good. I don't know what was worse: the dentist's drilling or my mind rushing to guess what horrible demise had befallen this mystery dog.

On the drive home Mother told me how she had agreed to adopt the drop-off and then had tied him up at the doghouse in the barn until she could figure out something better for him. The doghouse was comfortable and dry, lined with hay and old blankets, and it was positioned inside the barn near the large open sliding door so that a dog could go in and out as desired. There was also an open barn window high above the doghouse, alongside the open door.

The dog had only been there a few hours when a neighbor pulled up the driveway to the farmhouse and asked my mother, "Did you know that you have a dog hanging out your barn window?" Mortified, Mother ran down to the barn to discover that the dog had jumped on top of his doghouse and then out the high window above it. The poor thing had choked to death on his leash, even though he could easily have walked out the large barn door next to his doghouse if he'd wanted to be outside.

It was funny, the way that dog stayed with me, even though I'd never met him or even known what he looked like. I imagined a scraggly mutt, tail between his legs, and thought how being passed between three homes in one day must have been too much for any dog to handle. I wished I'd had the chance to show him how much he could be loved. I thought of him every time I saw that window, trying to guess why he would have taken that leap unless he was truly in distress. He must have felt so lonely.

I wish he could know that someone still thinks of him now.

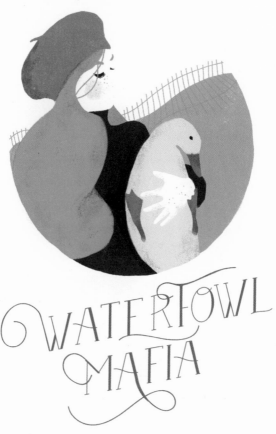

WATERFOWL MAFIA

S ome animals, like Mother's goose, Silly, have no
intention of being loved; in fact, they prefer may-
hem. And the fact that Silly eventually got re-
moved from the farm was entirely his own fault,
though he didn't seem to care much either way.

One spring Mother brought home three mallards

and an Indian Runner duck as a surprise for me. Though only one mallard was female and was able to earn her keep laying eggs, Mother did not complain since they brought me so much joy. I suppose they qualified more as pets than farm animals by our new, more relaxed farm rules.

My ducks were a bit shy, but while they were young they recognized me as their mother, following me around the farm in a line and eating watermelon out of my hand. Occasionally I would bring them inside to run around in the kitchen because the sound of their webbed feet smacking the kitchen floor made me laugh. Of course I never let them roam the carpeted areas of the house, as beat-up as those rugs already were from the constant traffic of ten dirty farm children, because of the ducks' complete lack of bladder control.

We all got along just fine until my mother introduced a new bird into the mix: a yellow baby goose. I hated geese, but Mother adored them for some reason that always escaped me. My aunt had flocks of geese that roamed loose on her farm, and when I worked in her blueberry fields picking berries to sell at the farm market, they would chase me out of the rows, flapping their giant wings and hissing.

Their ridged beaks meant painful bites, and even at my quickest I found their long necks difficult to outmaneuver.

But Mother was delighted with her baby goose. She named him Silly, though personally I thought Jerk would have been a much more suitable name for a goose—and this one in particular. When she introduced the gosling into the gang, the ducks were nearly full-grown and didn't much care for the newbie. But he was persistent. He followed them around, chirping, even though the ducks harassed the little fellow, putting his head into their mouths when he annoyed them, as if to say, "Shut up." Silly's stubbornness must have impressed them, though, because as soon as he grew into a full-sized white goose, they accepted him as their leader and followed him around without question wherever he went.

Geese had always had the reputation for attacking things, but ducks had not, as far as I knew. The goose clearly thought he was one of the ducks, but the ducks took on gooselike qualities, becoming more aggressive and even louder than before. Silly was much braver than they were; like most geese, he would attack me, hissing, so I would grab his beak and snap it shut with my hands, careful to dodge the sharp ridges on his beak. This would put him in such a fury that he would shake with anger, and when I eventually had to let go, he would stretch out his long neck and goose me on the butt as I ran away. The ducks watched and learned, and before long, if we turned our backs to the duck flock, they would start to chase after us too. But then as soon as we turned to look at them, they would scatter and act casual, as though they were up to nothing at all, quacking to each other in a conversational sort of way.

Still, I loved my misguided little cowards. While I sat cuddling one, the rest would gather nearby and murmur under their breaths to each other like they were planning a rescue mission. Inevitably I would release the duck from my arms when it pooped on me, though I'm not sure if that was part of their escape plan.

The ducks were much more aggressive with cars. At first, when Joel would pull up the driveway in his old white car after filling milk jugs at the neighbor's, the ducks would attack the car, and he would have to get out multiple times to shoo them off the driveway so he could park. Joel was convinced the goose thought his car was another large white goose threatening his territory. But it turned out they weren't just after Joel's car. Weeks passed, and as their boldness grew I began hearing cars honking and slowing down in the road. When I would travel all the way down the long driveway to investigate, I never saw anything suspicious—until one day when I was in the overgrown field across the road with Rachel's half-blind pony, Duke, whom I had put out to pasture in the tall grass.

It was a beautiful evening, and I knew I would need to drag him a little to persuade him to come in. I began leading Duke up to the barn, always walking on his good side, of course, when I heard a car come to a stop on the road. As I got closer, I realized Silly had stepped out into the middle of the road right in front of a jeep, trying to look as big as possible and squawking loudly, either as a threat to the jeep or as a signal to the ducks to do what they did next. Each of the four ducks jumped onto the road too and attacked the jeep's wheels, quacking as they pecked at the rubber. It looked like a drill, one I suspected they had been perfecting for days.

The couple in the jeep, who seemed like city people, laughed loudly, but I was mortified. My cheeks turned bright red, and I dropped my pony's rope, running to shoo away the interlopers. Once I'd managed to clear the road of the fowl, tucking a couple of the ducks under my arm and kicking toward the others to direct them back to the barn, I glanced behind me, wondering why I hadn't heard the jeep move. Duke, whose rope I had dropped in order to chase off the ducks, was now parked in front of the jeep, staring at them blankly with his one good eye. So I tossed the two ducks in the direction of the barn and ran to grab the pony, dodging the infuriated goose as I went.

Sadly even the waterfowl mafia, as we began calling them, wasn't immune to larger predators that were perhaps more cunning than cars. Early one morning, just before the sun rose, Father heard a commotion in the barn all the way from up at the farmhouse. The goose sounded the alarm, squawking loudly, and the ducks quacked frantically in a higher octave than usual. Father grabbed his shotgun and stomped down to the barn, where he found a fox in the duck pen, slim enough that it had been able to slip through a small gap between the chicken wire and the roof, which it had pried apart. The fox dashed off, leaving one of the mallards severely injured. I woke up to the sound of the gunshot that put the duck out of his misery.

The female mallard was not physically injured but acted flustered for the rest of her life. Traumatized, I guess. Her feathers always looked disheveled, even puffed. Eventually we lost the other two drakes to cars passing the farm, as I was never able to break them of the habit of attacking the wheels. The goose and one shell-shocked, overcautious duck remained.

Then our duck population grew by one when I adopted Robespierre, a white duck who needed a new home. Robespierre was ugly—one of those Muscovy ducks with caruncles on their face like a turkey. We used to call them "chicken-ducks" when we saw them swarming all over an abandoned farm we'd pass along the country roads on our morning drive—dubbed the "chicken-duck and flying plastic bag farm" since from what we could tell, that was exactly what it farmed.

Robespierre was a sweet lap duck and enjoyed one-on-one time just like a cat would. But ultimately it was her fearlessness that put her in danger. Silly the goose squished Robespierre to death in what I am guessing was an act of misguided romantic passion. After all, he thought he was a duck too. I picked up Robespierre's stiff, flattened body out of the vegetable garden where I'd found her and gave her the proper burial she deserved.

I had had enough of this farm bully. While the incident with Robespierre was the nail in Silly's coffin for me, it wasn't until he tormented my toddler niece that Mother was ready to say good-bye. My eldest sister, Becky, and her daughter were visiting on their summer break when Silly went after little Katie in the yard, flapping his wings and honking. The sheer terror on her face as she ran from the giant bird that was probably larger than she was could almost have been amusing if he hadn't goosed her on the butt. She broke out into dramatic sobs, and at that point Mother decided enough was enough.

Mother sent the goose and traumatized mallard to live on my aunt's farm the next town over; it happened behind my back when I wasn't home, as these transactions usually did. But in this case I knew it was for the best, and I was more than happy for Silly to be gone. Later, when I asked my aunt about the goose, she said he had bonded with four loose ducks instead of joining the other roaming geese, and they terrorized the road together. Eventually Silly died in battle with a car, as he would have liked.

WILD BIRDS

Mother's favorite farm animals were no doubt the barnyard birds, like chickens and geese. But she also had a special place in her heart for the wild birds that gathered in the branches outside the house. Every fall, Canadian geese would honk as they slowly crossed the sky, and for a day a mass of thousands of chirping blackbirds would descend on the farm, hopping from branch to branch like our place was a rest stop along their journey south.

The winter birds that came to our feeder were even more appreciative, as our winters were harsh and food was scarce when the snow was deepest. Mother felt it was her duty to feed all these hungry winter birds and delighted in seeing them congregate outside the windows while she went about her daily chores. Every holiday we knew exactly what to buy for her: more birdseed or another feeder. She hung so many bird feeders that you could see birds from nearly every window of the house.

Mother loved to listen to the birds, enjoying their songs as though they were her favorite hymns. She watched their patterns too, recognizing families and tracking the off-spring as they grew up and became independent. Then she would tell us around the dinner table what the bird families were up to, as though they were her dear friends.

I'd heard kids at school talk about how their mothers liked to watch soap operas; mine didn't watch TV, but I suppose some of the drama she saw unfold in those branches around the feeders wasn't far off. The bird feeder was the

center hub of bird activity. Grackles would greedily domi-
nate a particular feeder, while cardinals and other larger
birds would peck and poke for the best seed. The commotion was so noisy that it would attract the occasional hawk,
which would sweep down and snatch a dove or sparrow
from time to time. Meanwhile inside the dining room window, just a few feet from the largest feeder, house cats gathered to watch all the activity, their tails twitching.

I will always treasure how Mother surrounded
herself with birds. To me, they were sent from heaven to
bring her peace. I too knew the pain and loss that came
with loving and losing in the harsh environment of a farm,
and I saw it take its toll on her just as it did on me. I had my
cats, or "fuzz therapy," as I called it, to comfort me; Mother
had the songs of her birds.

PRECIOUS

*P*recious was our first blue jay. He came to live
with us one winter after a snowstorm so heavy
that the hemlocks were bent over with snow.
That in itself wasn't unusual; our valley was
close enough to Lake Erie that we would get particularly
harsh winters from the lake effect, with deeper snow and

earlier winters than in the city sixty miles to the south.

Joel was coming up from doing his chores in the barn when he recognized the squawk of a distressed baby blue jay in the distance. Following the sound over the noise of the snow and ice crunching under his boots, he trudged along until he saw the tiny bird, nearly naked of down feathers, sitting crying on the snow under the crab apple tree. Joel carefully delivered the baby to our mother's warm hands in the kitchen, and she immediately sent us for her Audubon rescue book. We mixed canned dog food with egg yolk, water, and vitamins and fed the bird constantly throughout the day and night.

Typically baby birds were hard to keep alive because they required such persistent feeding and care; compared to a kitten or puppy they were tiny, so fragile. Mother told me she would call the blue jay Precious because it was a miracle such a tiny thing survived after falling out of his nest, newly hatched, and she was determined to save him.

To our surprise, Precious recovered and grew quickly. When spring came, he had gained most of his adult feathers, so Mother would place him in the weeping willow tree outside the kitchen door while we worked in the garden. Precious would hop from branch to branch and await my mother's hand to feed him when he called for her, though he began cautiously exploring the outdoors a little farther every week. Fortunately his bright-blue wings were easy to spot, so we were able to keep a general eye on where he was.

Before long Precious had full rein of the farm, and I remember him flying freely through the house and in and out as he pleased. Precious did a perfect imitation of the microwave beep, causing my mother to check for finished food—she never seemed able to tell the difference between the machine's sound and Precious's pitch-perfect *beep beep beep*. I suspect Precious enjoyed our giggling after Mother realized she once again had fallen for the bird's prank.

Blue jays are playful and curious birds, drawn to anything stringlike or shiny. Once when the telephone company was working down at the bottom of our driveway, the repair tech knocked on the front door and asked Mother if she owned a pet blue jay. Mother feared the worst, of course, but he merely said, "Will you please come get him?" Apparently Precious was pulling at the electrical wires in the back of the truck and having a wonderful time. Mother went down, apologized on behalf of her bird, and carried the troublemaker inside the house.

Mother knew that just like with most pranksters, if Precious was out of sight for too long, she should probably go look for him. On one of these rounds her instincts took her down the hill to the barn. There, hanging upside down by one foot from a hemlock branch, was Precious, who had found a red string, God knows where, and played with it until he somehow managed to tangle it around his foot. Mother untangled her ridiculous bird, thankful she'd found him before he could hurt himself. From then on I made sure to collect stray bits of hay baler twine from around the yard and hide it from the irresponsible blue jay, though inevitably Precious would find new trouble elsewhere on the farm.

By the time fall came Precious was much bolder, and there was no corner of the farm he didn't know. In fact, he even began visiting with other blue jays on the property, and I often wondered what stories he told them about his life with his family of humans. But no matter how far he traveled, he would always come find Mother when she called for him or when he wanted some extra attention.

Mornings he would perch in a tree down by the

road and watch for the school bus, but after we left he usually flew back up to the house to visit my mother in the gardens and house throughout the day. One day Precious's curiosity got the best of him, and instead of heading to the house, he followed the school bus into town. He tailed the bus for six miles, but when it made its routine stop in Hallville, Precious became distracted by a bird feeder and decided to see what else the nice lady living there had to offer.

Two days went by, and Mother grew frantic. She paced the perimeter of the farm, calling for Precious and scanning trees for signs of a tangled bird or a stray black-and-blue feather. Every horrible possibility entered her mind—he'd been hit on the road or eaten by a cat, or maybe he was lost and unable to find food. Everyone could see she was distracted and distressed.

The morning of the second day, while Mother was once again out calling for her missing loved one, she stopped to get the mail. Among the assorted bills, junk mail, and newspapers, something caught her attention: on the front page of one newspaper was a picture of a woman sharing a bowl of ice cream with a blue jay! It was Precious, of course, obviously enjoying himself and making new friends.

Seeing that picture of him being spoiled in another home, I felt betrayed, even if I was glad he was safe and having a grand time on his new adventure. Fear of his death was replaced by fear of him moving on. But not for long, because the very next afternoon he flew home to us, wild with excitement. We could hear him coming up from the bottom of the farm, calling triumphantly, announcing himself and demanding that we open the door.

Precious was more excited than we'd ever seen him, like he was trying to tell us all about his adventures. He circled the house, practically yelling. He flew up and down the stairs, Mother following him, certain he was going to hurt himself in all that excitement. As Mother descended the stairs she called out to Marla, who had just gotten home from school, "Do you see Precious down there?" Marla said no, but as Mother turned the corner out of the stairwell hall, she stepped on him, not realizing he had landed on the carpet to rest.

Mother was heartbroken. She picked up her pet, who was breathing very slowly, scarcely moving. His eyes glazed over. Retreating into the privacy of the pantry, she cradled her bird as he died over a few long minutes. It was the only time we youngest kids had ever heard our mother cry.

Mother speaks fondly about Precious to this day, repeating how thankful she is for her time with him. But following Precious's death she threw herself into her work with more determination than ever, and for many years after, her guilt over his death would present itself in a small comment or lament, the pain still freshly evident.

It wasn't until much later that I realized this was only partly about Precious and more about what had happened before our parents moved the eldest three children to the farm—the point at which everything changed for our family.

Peter was my older brother, born after Paul—child number four. I had heard that Peter was a SIDS death, but it was something we never discussed, especially around Mother. Many years later, details surfaced: one cold winter morning a couple months after Peter was born, Mother discovered he had died during the night. I heard stories about Mother falling over the small casket in fits of sobbing, then becoming lethargic and despondent for months, full of questions, regrets, and ever-present pain.

At that time my family lived in a very small house in Zelienople. Father was teaching and pursuing his doctorate while Mother raised their small children and ran the household on their modest income. Stretched thin already and facing the grief of loss himself, Father grew deeply worried about Mother. As it happened, around this time Mother's sister and her husband bought a farm in the country, and shortly afterward another farm a ways down the road went up for sale. Father believed that the best thing to do was to escape the cramped house in Zelienople, which held so many bad memories. He moved the family to the farm, where Mother could recover and get her hands into the dirt, like she so loved to do. There they banished the cruel outside world and the old neighbors who only looked on in pity, reminding my parents of their loss. The farm was a chance for a new beginning.

Mother needed the healing influence of the farm, and the ancient farmhouse needed a strong, young family to keep it. The land itself needed nature lovers who would appreciate and rehabilitate its beauty. The animals needed a family to love and care for them. I suppose we were the perfect fit, the appointed caretakers who gave and received back. You could say the farm was birthed out of death: Peter's. But that somehow seemed fitting, given the never-ending cycle of life, death, and love I experienced during my existence there. Each new kitten and puppy, with a fresh and fragile look on life, inspired joy and awe, and though the death of the innocent was often hard to accept, it only seemed to give the times of joy a more three-dimensional aspect. These new lives were something to be appreciated, treasured, and protected. The tough, self-sacrificial drive was the natural and right response to these new and dreadful dimensions of joy and pain.

When Peter was put in the ground, Mother brought forth a dizzying array of life from the earth. And remembering Mother's hands deep in the soil of the farm, every season bringing about a new cycle of life in her gardens—and the peace in her face as she worked with the land and took the bird songs to heart—I know Father made the right call in bringing her there.

BUDDELIA

When I was thirteen, the school nurse sent a note home for my parents: "Elisabeth has scoliosis." Mother and Father didn't think much of it, since a number of my siblings and my mother herself had slight curves to their spines. Jesse's even curved in a way that made his chest sink in.

Besides, because I was one of the youngest of so many children, my parents had become a bit more relaxed, not running to the doctor at every scare. I had a number of ailments that had gone unattended for longer than perhaps they would have in other families, yet I seemed otherwise fine.

But the scoliosis was a lingering problem. And by the time I was fifteen, my spine had twisted quite severely into an *S*.

That year I was heading down to the creek in my bathing suit when Mother caught a glimpse of my back and stopped me for a closer look, alarmed by how quickly it had worsened. She and Father took me to a children's hospital, which recommended surgery; it was too late for a back brace. But Father had done his research and heard from many sources how horrible the operation could be—how my mobility would be changed for the rest of my life and that I would most likely become dependent on painkillers. Father, hoping for a less extreme option than spinal fusion, told the doctor we needed to think about it.

I don't know how my parents found the time, but they explored every other option. They took me to faith healers as far away as Toronto and Florida, with no success. I concluded my faith was too weak and felt bad for wasting their time. We visited a chiropractor, whose invention resembled a medieval torture rack: I lay down on my stomach, weights on my back, my outstretched arms holding on to handles while the machine stretched me out. It was painful and largely ineffective, but the chiropractor taught me a breathing trick for managing the pain, and that I used for years afterward.

One of Father's articles suggested I sleep on my back in bed with books stacked under the curved part of my spine. This was so uncomfortable, even painful, though, that I couldn't fall asleep. Father showed me a video for pain management that walked me through navigating my way to an imaginary pain control panel in my brain. I pictured turning down the pain with a lever while practicing breathing exercises, and it helped me through many sleepless nights.

Around this time I realized that Marla, compassionate almost to a fault, was extremely concerned for me. When I was in the bath, she would knock on the door and ask if she could come in to wash my back. Marla would sit on the mat, tending to my back with a washcloth and singing softly. She knew the bath had always been my comfort place. I thought back to how Mother had consoled both of us in that same bathtub after Orangie's death. It was funny how when I was surrounded by warm water, things felt so much more optimistic.

We tried alternative treatments for months, but they only added to my discomfort. I did not care that I looked like something out of a sideshow at an old-fashioned circus. But I could no longer stand for longer than five minutes without great pain and difficulty breathing. I couldn't lift my flute without my spine hurting or blow into my instrument without becoming short of breath. I couldn't run on the farm either, or spend as much time roaming its grounds with the animals. I could barely participate in gym class. Defeated, Mother and Father drove me back to the children's hospital, and the doctors told us it was time for spinal fusion. And right away; apparently the twisting of the spine was also moving my ribs and putting pressure on or even shifting organs like my heart and lungs. That sounded about right. I could feel painful squeezing in my upper torso and a deep ache all the way down my spine and into my legs.

At this point I was sixteen years old, and I was more than ready. The morning I was to go to the hospital, I said good-bye to my dog Buddelia, my constant companion for the past few years, and cuddled all the cats while Mother promised there would be nothing for me to worry about in their regard. I wasn't sure what people packed to take to a hospital, but I put some things in an old bag and stashed it in the van. I was anxious about the trip. I didn't know how my life was going to change, what I would be like after I got back, or even when that would be.

Then I heard what sounded like five or six motorcycles coming down our usually quiet country road, descending into our valley with loud sputtering. When they turned to climb up our driveway, I recognized the boy in front as one of Marla and Rachel's friends, Rob. I had adopted his duck, Robespierre, when he and his mother could no longer care for her, so perhaps this was his thank you. It turned out that when my sisters had seen the list of things I would never be allowed to do again post-operation, like riding roller coasters, skiing, carrying heavy things, and skydiving, they had also seen motorcycles on the list. After discussing it with their friends, they had planned one last pre-operation adventure: my first-ever motorcycle ride.

I have to admit I was terrified as I climbed on the back of Rob's bike and we took off, faster than I was sure was safe, along the country roads. They had plotted out the route with the steepest hills, which we hit at such high speeds that I wasn't sure if I could hold on. We passed farms I'd never seen, the cows turning their heads to see what the loud engines were. On some particularly terrifying hills I wondered if I would even survive to get the operation. Then I found I was smiling, even laughing as we raced all the way back to the farm.

I climbed off the bike, saying a bashful thank you, and rejoined Marla, who had asked to come along to the hospital. My parents were also waiting by the van. It was clear from their faces that they had been in on the secret too. I was surprised they had allowed it. But as the bikes left and we hit the road as well, I realized I was no longer afraid of what lay ahead.

That evening I sat in my hospital bed, quietly pondering what the next morning would bring. We knew it was going to be an eight-hour surgery and that there was risk of paralysis. I tried my best to curl up into a ball in case it was the last time I would be able to bend my back, trying to fix the feeling and the experience in my memory.

Watching me, Marla began to cry. We had always been very different; I never wanted to talk about feelings and didn't always know how to handle the hugs she showered me with. But during much of my time in the hospital, Marla wouldn't leave my side, even though she was starting college at a very challenging school. Of course there was always that unspoken rule in our family—it was your responsibility to care for your next youngest sibling. But up until this point I had been the one to keep an eye on her, since she was more sensitive.

I could remember sitting at the top of the stairs, listening to her cry in her room. I was no good with words and awkward with physical affection, so I would sit and wait, not sure what to do. It wasn't like with my animals, whose needs were more black and white; my older teenage sister had me stumped. Inevitably, though, I would knock softly on her door, walk in, and just sit with her, maybe put my hand on her knee or give her a hug and let her cry. She seemed to understand this was the best I could offer, and maybe she took comfort in that. During particularly dark times for her, I would guard the outside of her bedroom door or lie next to her at night, afraid she might run away from our farm if I didn't keep close watch. She called me the tough one, but when it was my turn to be weak, she was anxious to be there for me.

The operation was successful, other than nerve damage blanketing the ribs on my right side, where the hunch had been. But nothing felt right to me. The days moved in slow motion, a few seconds at a time, as I fought the overwhelming pain. I tried holding my breath so the ache lessened, but then alarms would go off next to my bed, and frustrated, tired nurses would rush into my room with their blinding flashlights, scolding me: "Beth, you have to breathe!" I remember looking up at Marla's face as she wiped mine with a warm cloth. She had tears in her eyes again, seeing me in such pain. In that moment I thought of the cats we'd had to put out of their misery. I wondered if she could tell.

Eventually I was moved from intensive care into a shared room with three other children. As the pain less-ened, my vision shifted beyond my self-pity. The first night in my shared room, I heard what to this day puts tears in my eyes: a tiny voice down the hall crying, "I want to go home," then another voice crying the same thing. And another: "I want my mommy." From what I could tell, these cries came from children as young as three or four years old. It was far sadder than the cry of any sick kitten. I wanted to run to these little kids and tell them they weren't alone, but I was still bedbound.

When I was healed enough to stand, a nurse would guide me slowly to the end of the hall and back, and one day I was allowed to walk all the way to the board game room. This was a small room with shelves of board games and two double glass doors overlooking a lawn area with sidewalks, and when I stepped inside, I realized how long it had been since I had seen the outdoors or felt sun on my skin. I ached for the farm. I felt like a mouse in a terrarium. And then I realized there was one other child in the room, a small boy of about six. He was in some sort of custom reclining wheel-chair, and he looked up at me and said, "Outside?" I stared at him as he repeated it in a sad voice that haunts me even now.

How had he even gotten into the game room? I

didn't think he had the strength to wheel himself, certainly not a complex chair like that. I tried explaining to him that he needed to ask a nurse, that I wasn't allowed to take him outside, but he didn't seem to understand. It was possible that outside was one of the only English words he knew. Choked up, I left the room and returned to my bed.

That day I realized that at sixteen I was the oldest patient there, and that the Shriners who ran the facility were paying for everything. My heart swelled. This meant a lot, as my parents had recently filed for bankruptcy. But from what I could tell, the other children there came from even poorer families than mine, and their parents could not afford to take time off work to be there with them. When my large family gathered around my bed, I felt loved, but also horrible for the small children who watched alone from their beds. I must not have been the only one to feel guilt over this, because the next time Mother arrived she had gifts and plenty of love to share with the other children down my hall. She even brought fruit from the farm market, which of course was inspected by hospital staff before she distributed each small bag to an excited child.

Now that a piece of the farm had finally come to

me, something felt right again. I got updates on my pets. And Father, knowing I missed them, had even brought me a pocket-sized electronic game in the shape of a cat's head— something he had found at the gas station on their drive to visit me. It was a digital pet that I had to feed and water from my hospital bed.

I was so ready to see my real creatures, especially my dog Buddelia, who was becoming more tired in her old age. When Buddelia had shown up on the farm years earlier, Mother had told me not to feed her, so that she would go away. Naturally I couldn't resist giving her a slice of bologna in secret, and that's when she decided to stay and be my dog—just as Mother had feared she would. I remember going to the grocery store to buy a collar and some dog food, debating with my little brother over what to call the new arrival. Mother suggested Buddy, and that name stuck until the day Buddy had puppies. I hadn't even realized she was female, let alone pregnant. It was then that Father suggested renaming her Buddelia. By the time I had my surgery, we'd been companions for years, and more than ever I longed to roam the farm with my beloved pet. But at this point I could barely walk on my own.

When Mother and Father were finally allowed to bring me home, it took two people to lift me into the front seat of the van. They packed pillows all around me, but I remember how the bumps in the parking lot, even though we were going at a snail's speed, sent shocks of pain through my body. I still couldn't turn my head, but I strained my eyes to see the children's hospital as we left, to fix it into my memory...the bad, the good, the deep appreciation. That's when I saw something that made me understand my stay a little better.

Outside one side door on a stoop sat three nurses on their smoke break. None of them spoke. They just stared into space, frowning and puffing on their cigarettes. I realized how hard their jobs had to be, seeing suffering, homesick children every day, hearing them cry at night. Of course that would take its toll. Earlier, these women had seemed callous to me, but I knew I could not do better. Nothing I did on the farm for my animals could compare to what they did every day. I felt like the most useless person on earth. But I also felt challenged to be more compassionate and to keep doing my part to help others, whether person or pet.

I began the transition to staying at home, though

the healing was slow. The removal of my rib—part of the operation—had irritated one of my lungs, which then filled with fluid, and when the pressure of the fluid became intolerable, I knew I had to go back to the hospital. But I insisted on waiting until I'd had the chance to say good-bye to Buddelia. My beloved dog, with whom I'd been so looking forward to sharing adventures again, had developed pneumonia and probably wouldn't last until I was able to come home.

I couldn't let Buddelia slip away, no matter how much pain I was in. So Marla helped me get out of bed, and I walked slowly and carefully to find my dog. I had never felt so fragile in my life. Cats rubbed against my feet, as if it was their turn to comfort me. I had missed them, but right now my heart needed to see Buddelia.

I continued my slow walk of the farm, stopping to catch my breath a few times, until I found Buddelia on the grass outside the giant sliding doors of the upstairs barn. I struggled to get down to my knees to pet my companion, not sure if I would be able to get back up on my own, and I talked to her for a while. Buddelia was having difficulty breathing because of the pneumonia, but I could also see she had a deep gash in her throat from our jealous dog Star, a dropped-off pit bull–wiener. I remember telling Buddelia that the symptoms she suffered were much like what I was experiencing from the fluid around my lungs. She slowly wagged her tail while I petted her, and I felt a kinship with her as we enjoyed each other's company, though melancholy, both of us struggling through painful breaths. I thought surely I could be brave and stay positive if my beagle could.

The next day Mother came to my bedroom, sat me up, and told me that Buddelia had passed away. Mother assured me she had sat with my dog while Buddelia labored to breathe awhile and then stopped breathing altogether. I thanked her for being with Buddelia and promised her I was fine. I tried hard not to think about my dog's death and how I hadn't been there for her. Not to think about the pain she had been in at the end. But I had to cry and then sob, and then the sobbing became more about the pain in my lungs and spine from the heaving than anything else.

I never fully got to finish mourning Buddelia that day, but I chose to be thankful that at least she wasn't suffering any longer. And the next day at the hospital, as soon as the needle entered my lung, I felt instant relief too. With every drip of the yellow, frothy fluid that drained from around my lungs—nearly filling a two-liter container—I could breathe better and without pain. I was so happy that I barely noticed the new pain in my hand, which I had sprained squeezing a nurse's hand while the needle was pushed between my ribs. I apologized to the nurse and she smiled at me kindly, glad the procedure had worked.

When the bandage was taken off my spine sometime later, Marla asked me if I would like to see how my fixed back looked. It was quite the transformation. Though far from perfect—I realized I would never have a completely symmetrical back—it was worlds different from the deformity I had had before. And better still, running down almost the entire length of my spine was a thick red scar, my badge of bravery. I had never hoped to look flawless or beautiful, only strong and brave and perhaps unique. Seeing that scar and my new back, I smiled, proud beyond words. I felt more able to face whatever life might bring to me, and I knew I was ready to make my last farewells to my beloved Buddelia.

Mother had planted a small garden on Buddelia's

grave in the cemetery, and once I had recovered a little more, I went to visit and sat in the soft grass with my dog for a long while. The ribbon grass was already spreading across the cemetery hillside—Buddelia's life transferred through the fertile soil into a living thing again. I felt the grass softly brush my legs then, and every time I visited the graveyard or traveled down to the creek to swim. It reminded me of the feel of her soft fur against my leg, back when she was my constant companion. In those moments it felt like she, and all the beloved pets we had buried there, was still with me in some small way.

PLACE OF PEACE

I marvel at how much has changed over the years our family has lived on the farm. Back in the time of my oldest siblings, before I was born, our larger livestock were slaughtered on the farm and their bones and entrails dumped in the woods, far back from the barn. Stripped by scavengers and bleached by time and the sun, these bones were later gathered up and hung in trees, props to terrify our unsuspecting cousins on midnight hikes into the swamp. With a quick flick of the flashlight beam at a well-timed moment, we could illuminate the hovering bony apparition, to the terror of our city tourists.

The boneyard once creeped us younger children out, especially if we were near it as a fog rolled in. Now that area serves as a reminder of how the farm has evolved. My experience was very different from that of my eldest siblings, who witnessed the transition of our family onto the farm during our darkest time. During my later childhood I saw the farm shift once again as it wrestled with its purpose of survival and its growing reputation as a home for the bad-luck stories, the socially unacceptable critters, the unwanted and unfortunate. Our barnyard collective gave them, too, a second chance.

As I grew older and started college, Steve and Erica picked up the torch, taking on many of the responsibilities of caring for our farm creatures. For the first time it was possible for all our cats and dogs to be neutered and given their shots—or at least the ones we could catch. I did some small rescue missions while away at school, but Erica worked with various vets over the years, and through these jobs new misfit animals would make their way home with her almost constantly, keeping the spirit of the farm alive and full of hope. Eventually Steve and Erica purchased their own small farm, and there she gathered creatures of their own: antisocial cats that did not fit in regular homes, a three-legged chinchilla that'd had an accident on a running wheel, a one-eyed mouse, and an eyeless cat, to name just a few.

As things are bound to happen, I grew up and pursued a career in the city, but I could not go far, settling a little over an hour away. And when the family's luck took a hit, I grew into a new role, one of taking care of the farm that had taken care of me. With the farm market no longer able to compete with big box stores, I started a new family business that has allowed me, and my siblings who are involved in the business, to support our aging parents and cover the upkeep of an older farm.

It has been incredible to give back in a bigger, more meaningful way—to finally feel strong, a solution, a defender of the farm itself and not merely its smallest inhabitants. But my business has kept me traveling across the country, and sometimes I feel the separation from the land like a pain deep in my heart, as though a part of me is missing. And then I experience the comfort and wholeness of being home again each time I find my way back on weekends.

I still bring cat food, as well as more fanciful treats like toys and heated cat houses for the barn cats. And I still enjoy barn search expeditions and collecting armfuls of newborn kittens and taking brand-new ducklings, which are always designated as mine, down to the creek to learn to swim. But even when I'm not there, my motivation is to protect that sacred place. To fix it. To guard my family's hearts and the new generations of animals.

I like to look to the future of the farm, and I dream of moving back when I'm able, of building a house and studio in the field across the road from our farmhouse. In the meantime the joy I see now in my siblings' children stirs my heart and gives me hope for our family, our farm, and our future. I love watching them discover the land. There is that moment when one of them bonds to a creature, and my heart is pulled back to similar meetings that stopped time in their simplicity and truth and beauty. Sitting eye to eye with a kitten, our closeness speaking of love and understanding. Resting my head on a mother cat and letting her purr drown out the worries of the world. Running to greet a dog intent on knocking me down with joy when I finally finished my chores. Staring out the living room window, surprised that so much color could show up in a winter storm—the blustery bullying of blue jays, the regal red of the masked cardinals, and the plump juncos in their little suits of black and white, hoping to join the crowd in our huge homemade feeders. Who knew there could be so many shades of brown, or that when the light hit just right, bare branches could glow gold or crimson?

So much at our farm has changed, but the sense of wonder and the love go on. We still crowd there on weekends or for reunions, though the pace has slowed to a quieter beat—the fields no longer hold hay for harvesting, and the barns are relatively empty of life except for Mother's chickens, my ducks, and of course the ever-fluctuating numbers of cats. Dogs of all sizes still keep the cats in check and follow anyone looking to be going on an adventure. The big creatures have moved on, though deer still roam the woods, and bears visit now and then. The overgrown grasses and brush of the once-cultivated fields are home to plenty of wildlife.

Each season I am reminded of the depth of life that exists there on the land. Flocks of birds still visit our farm as they migrate, and the lonely magical calls of ducks resound in the far woods. New little red squirrels outrun the dogs and chitter angrily at the cats from high in the walnut trees, just as they did when I was a child. We now have mown paths through the overgrown fields to bring us in quicker contact with nature, and the grandkids crowd onto the four-wheeler and whip through the paths, jumping off at the swamp to peek around the old places we too once heard calling to us. The dogs buzz by or get in our faces for attention, then return to their imaginary hunts. We still find the lonely bones of wild things that succumbed to predators, the elements, or age. These unmarked and uncovered graves always draw my mind to the past buried deep in our farm and woods.

Too many times I look back and see the good, the love I've lost as my pets disappeared into my memories and the ground. Some of their unfortunate deaths are the things of nightmares, and many still break my heart. I will not deny that they have formed, pulled, pushed me into what

I am now, changed how I look at the world and experience it. I choose not to forget them or even my weaknesses or inability to help. In some ways I feel like I am still figuring out what their lives meant in their flickering time on the farm. I am privileged to have known them, but did they have to suffer? I am thankful for our time together, but could I have done more? I will continue to ask these questions as I tell their stories, and I think that will keep me honoring my fading friends' memories. I will remember them as we were together and allow my time with them as keeper, nurse, and companion to continue to shape my heart and head as I walk through my city home and on my frequent visits to the farm. I will continue to love even when it hurts.

The graveyard on the east hill above the creek is still there. Every so often a new marker appears, or an old one crumbles and disappears into the earth. Now that I'm older, the orchard in that spot looks a little less wild and untamed. But even now, below the old gnarled apple trees, the gently waving grasses amid the thorns give the place an air of peace.

BETH VOLTZ grew up surrounded by animals, but not merely those you'd expect on a struggling farm. Her home was that farm where people surreptitiously dropped off their unwanted, sick, even dying pets, leaving her family of twelve to care for them. Shoebox Funeral shares Beth's heartfelt stories about the farm she cherishes and the ducks, cats, dogs and birds that she befriended, knowing they wouldn't be around for very long.

IDIL GÖZDE graduated from the Art Institute of Fort Lauderdale with a Bachelor of Fine Arts degree in Graphic Design and Motion Graphics. She is an award winning multi-disciplinary artist who is known for her whimsical illustrations and love for lettering. She has crafted her way as an animator for many years and continues producing work designing through various platforms for compelling stories.

ACKNOWLEDGEMENTS

Thank you to my parents for giving me their love, the farm, and my ten siblings...the most important things in my life.

To my siblings, Marla, Renee, Rebecca, Jesse, Stephen, Peter, and especially Rachel, Joel, Paul, and Ray, for their tremendous help writing this book. Also for their help with my jewelry business, Ragtrader Vintage, so that we can continue to support the farm which is the heart of this book. Also to Kate, Nathan and Sean.

To the farm and its animals, for making me who I am.

Huge thanks to Erica, my sister-in-law, who has taken the medical care of our farm animals into her loving, extremely capable hands.

Thanks to Michael Killen, who urged me almost every week for thirteen years to write these memories down. I would never have started or finished this book without his kind prodding. Thank you for always believing in me.

And thanks to Animal Media Group for making this book possible and for being an inspiring place to work.

Also to Howard Shapiro for guiding me through the process with so much encouragement and patience.

Thanks to my editor, Christina M. Frey, for turning my giant mess of memories and feelings into something readable.

And to Idil for putting so much care and talent into illustrating and designing my book.

To John Hoberg for his awesome writing advice.

To Shriners Hospitals for Children, who performed my back surgery and saved my life.

And thank you for reading.

Dedicated to the loving memory of Peter, without whom we would never have come to the farm.

And to the memory of Francis the Ferret, whose sudden passing just one day before this book went to print reminded me once again how it feels to lay a precious animal friend to rest in the farm graveyard.

For more information please log onto

www.animalmediagroup.com

Please send your questions, comments or feedback to

info@animalmediagroup.com

Please follow me on Instagram

@shoeboxfuneral

PHOTO ALBUM

OUR BARN FROM ABOVE (1979)

Farm House

THE FIELD BEHIND OUR HOME

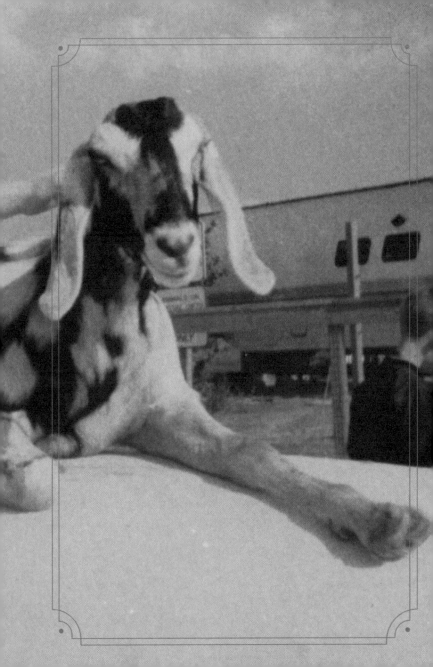

UNCLE CLARENCE, THE ROBOT

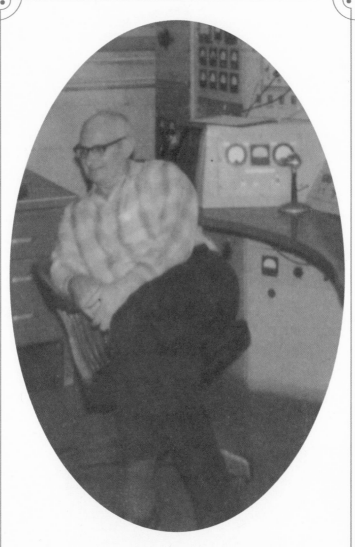

GRANDPA VOLTZ WORKING AT THE SYNCHROCYCLOTRON

CATS AT THE DOOR

PRECIOUS

DUKE

Lazy Rabbits

Buddelia

MOTHER AND FATHER

MOTHER AND FATHER

JOURNAL

JOURNAL

JOURNAL

JOURNAL

JOURNAL

JOURNAL